WERE YOU THERE?

WERE YOU THERE?
People of Christ's Passion

ROSS SAUNDERS

MOREHOUSE PUBLISHING

Morehouse Publishing
P.O. Box 1321
Harrisburg, PA 17105

Morehouse Publishing is a division of The Morehouse Group.

Cover design by Corey Kent

Cover photo by William K. Geiger of mural by Jan Henrik DeRosen,
Joseph of Arimathea Chapel, Washington National Cathedral

Printed in the United States of America

Saunders, Ross.
    Were you there? : people of Christ's passion / Ross Saunders.
        p.   cm.
    Includes bibliographical references (p.).
    ISBN 0-8192-1816-2 (pbk.)
    1. Jesus Christ Biography—Passion Week. 2. Apostles Biography.
3. Bible. N.T. Biography. I. Title.
BT414.S28 1999
232.96—dc21   99-31069
                                                          CIP

Contents

This book is based upon Lenten studies I was asked to lead at Christ's Church Lavender Bay in Sydney, Australia.

For a number of years I had been studying insights that cultural anthropologists had brought to the understanding of the people among whom Jesus lived and worked and taught. This helped me to decide to focus on some of the people—men and women, named and unnamed, followers and enemies—who were crucial to Jesus as he faced his inevitable death during the final days of his life as a human being on earth.

These people were Mediterraneans: Jews, Greeks, and Romans. Because they lived in a time different from our own, they had a completely different way of understanding the world and their place in it. Far too often we project our world and our ideas back onto those who lived in biblical times and thus misunderstand much of what was going on. We need to try to get inside their heads and their hearts if we are ever to come to terms with the dynamics of the gospel narratives.

The human Jesus, also a Mediterranean, was as much in need of the understanding and support of friends as any other person faced with the pressure of inevitable doom. He would have needed people around him: people who would understand his needs, people who would support him and stand beside him, people who would be prepared to give up their own cares and worries to be there for him.

This is a book about a man discovering who his real friends were, a man discovering the fickleness of human friendship, a man crying out for human companionship, a man soon to hang on a Roman cross for the sin of the whole of humanity, a man let down by his best and most trusted friends. It is also a book about the unlikely heroes and heroines who unexpectedly came out of the woodwork and helped Jesus realize that all was not lost, that there were some people who, when it really counted, brought encouragement and strength when they were sorely needed.

This book is dedicated to those who listened to me and learned what a brutal death crucifixion actually was and just what Jesus must have gone through during those last few days on earth. Bringing to others Jesus and the people he had to deal with helped me, more than I can possibly say, to relate our faith today to the people and the events surrounding the most unjust and cruel death of an innocent man ever perpetrated in the whole of human history.

I have included resources of readings and discussion questions that may be of help whether you are using this book in a discussion group or for your own Lenten reading. In these later years of my own life and Christian experience, I have found it vitally important to spend some time each Lenten season coming to terms with the reality of the crucifixion that Jesus deliberately endured in order to rescue each one of us from the power and corrupting influence of sin in our lives. That involves trying to understand something of the shame, pain, and reality of being deserted by trusted friends.

If we are ever to comprehend the meaning of the events of that first Easter, we must try to view the world through the eyes of the men and women who lived in Jesus' day. Consider this example from John's Gospel: After his resurrection, Jesus appeared to the disciples in the upper room. In John 20:22 we read: "[Jesus] breathed

on them and said to them, 'Receive the Holy Spirit.'"
How often have you read or heard those words? But have
you ever wondered what the reaction of those eleven
men would have been to having Jesus' breath blown
directly onto their faces? In fact, they would have
recoiled in shock. To them it was as though Jesus had
spat upon them, and that was one of the most humiliat-
ing things a person could do to another in those days.
Today we have a bad reaction to another person's breath
on our faces only if they have halitosis. But, for
Mediterraneans of Jesus' day, this encounter was not
about bad breath. Instead, it was about being humiliated.

To understand what their reactions would have been
we must understand their concepts of in-placeness and
out-of-placeness. As you read this book you will come to
see that one of the main messages of this incident in
John's Gospel is that God often chooses things that dis-
gust us humans to convey the grace and mercy of God's
Spirit. God's will is not limited by our cultural sensitivi-
ties. If Jesus could eat and talk with prostitutes and
despised tax collectors, then God's healing Spirit can also
come to us through Jesus' human spittle mixed with dirt
and smeared on the eyes of our blindness. God's enliven-
ing Spirit can crash through the barriers of our Western
middle-classness and cultural triumphalism.

"Were you there when they crucified my Lord?" probes
the Negro spiritual. Yes, we were there as members of the
human race. But which members? His friends? Most of
them let him down. His enemies? They were bent on his
execution, though he was innocent of any crime whatsoever. The onlookers? They were voyeurs, feeding their
blood-lust on his dripping, scarlet blood. His followers?
Most of them deserted him when their cause was aban-
doned. His family? Only his mother stood beside him on
Calvary. Those who really did believe in him as Messiah?

But they did not see him die for them. To be there, we must try to get inside the heads and hearts of all those people before we can decide which ones we are today.

My hope is that this book will help you, too, to do just that.

Simon Peter and John

The only way we can understand what was involved for Peter and John, when Jesus called them to leave their fishing nets and follow him, is to understand the core social values that drove them and their fellow Jews.

Embedded Identity

The first core value in visualizing Peter and John as men of their day is "embedded identity." Simon, for example, could not say, as he would say had he lived in our day, "I am Simon. I am a fisherman. I have a wife and three children. I live in Capernaum where I am well known as one of the major suppliers of fish for that town." That, you see, presupposes that Simon thought of himself as a separate individual with an identity apart from everyone else in his village.

In Jesus' day no one knew himself or herself as a person separate from another person. People always saw themselves in relationship to some other significant person or household. To find out who you were, you asked someone else: you found out who you were from other people, not from inside yourself. And, in the household group that formed the basic unit of Mediterranean society, all household members were identified in relationship to the head of their household: "the son of...," "the wife of...," "the slave of...," "the daughter of...," "the day laborer of..." whoever was the household head.

Thus, Simon would say, "I am Simon son of Jonah, son of..., assisting my father in his family business of fishing. My father arranged my marriage with...with whom I

have sired three children. When my father dies I will succeed him as the head of his household. As head, I will be
responsible for the care of my mother, if she is still alive,
for finding suitable wives for any of my brothers not yet
married, for providing dowries and suitable husbands
for any of my sisters still in my father's household, and
for the supervision of the household slaves and seasonal
workers I have inherited."

Simon's identity comes from someone else, not from
his own ego. And that is how everyone else in the village
perceives him. He is Simon, son of Jonah the fisherman.

HONOR AND SHAME

The other core value that has to be understood is that of
honor and shame. In all Mediterranean societies, every
member of a household knew his or her position with
relationship to every other member. And every household head knew his status with relationship to every
other household head in the same village or city.

It was as though people journeyed through their lives
in a long status queue, always knowing who they were in
relationship to the one ahead and the one behind. Thus,
one's honor was the place in the status queue given by
the others in that queue. It was almost impossible to
jump ahead a place or two, but rather easy to go down a
place or two. If a man decided to go into the army,
served well, and returned to his village a hero, then he
was advanced a place or two. But if he decided to
become an athlete and always lost his races, then he
would go down a place or two.

People in Mediterranean societies, even the peasants
and day laborers, were extremely status conscious.

But with status came responsibilities. A landowner
would be expected to endow his community with gifts in

accord with his perceived status, and all such gifts were
publicly acknowledged. Any failure to meet these obligations would result in his being shamed. He would also be
required to entertain members of his own status level
with occasional feasts, and he would expect to be so
entertained in return.

Every household head had responsibilities toward his
entire household, including providing a suitable husband
and dowry for his daughters, finding a wife of suitable
status for his sons, and always acting in public in accord
with his status of honor. Should any member of a household commit any act in breach of his or her status level,
then the head of the household was blamed and was the
object of public dishonor. His wife was the chief monitor
of public behavior, making sure not only that she
behaved properly but also that her husband always
remembered his place and behaved accordingly.

You may remember that Mary played this role of
behavior monitor when chiding the twelve-year-old
Jesus for staying behind in Jerusalem without telling his
parents (Luke 2:41–52).

When the rich young ruler was told by Jesus to sell all
he had and give to the poor, he was being told to shame
himself before his whole community and the synagogue
of which he was the head. With no money left, the young
man would not have been able to meet his obligations to
his community and synagogue, resulting in his being
shamed. This is what he could not face, and he walked
away from Jesus (Mark 10:17–31; Matthew 19:16–30;
Luke 18:18–25).

Peter, as the inheriting son of his father—the joint
head with Zebedee of the village fishing business—would
have been rated as a small businessman in the status
scale of his village. This would place him just above
slaves, day laborers, and artisans. He would be expected,

when his father passed on, to continue to donate important items to the village council meeting house, synagogue, and port facilities, as well as to help subsidize local festivals and celebrations. He would be expected to arrange regular feasts for his social equals and in turn attend their feasts. He would be expected to dress in public as befitted his perceived place in the status queue.

When Jesus publicly called upon Peter to put down his nets and leave behind the fishing business and follow him into a nomadic and shameful homelessness and joblessness, he was asking him to dishonor his father, his father's household, his father's village, and his father's name as an honored benefactor, household head, father, and citizen of Capernaum. Peter brought no shame upon himself—only upon his father and his village.

In demanding this of Peter, Jesus was asking no more than he had demanded of himself when he left behind his widowed mother and unmarried brothers and sisters, shaming his dead father's name and his village of Nazareth. Only when we fully understand that core value of honor and shame can we ever begin to come to terms with what Jesus did when he began his mission and called those twelve men to follow his example.

But one day Jesus gave Simon a new name—a new identity. When Jesus asked his disciples to tell him who they believed he (Jesus) was, it was Simon who said, "You are the Messiah, the Son of the living God." Jesus' response was, "Blessed are you, Simon son of Jonah! For flesh and blood has not revealed this to you, but my Father in heaven" (Matthew 16:16–17).

Notice that Jesus affirmed that Simon still had his identity as the son of his father Jonah, even though he had lost it when he gave away his place in his father's household. Notice also that Jesus affirmed the identity Simon had given him as the son of his Father in heaven.

This was all strictly in accord with the way Mediterraneans saw their identity in relationship to someone else.

Next, Jesus gave Peter a new identity. "And I tell you, you are Peter [a piece of rock], and on this rock [foundation] I will build my church, and the gates of Hades will not prevail against it" (Matthew 16:18). Notice that he was not to be identified as "Peter son of..." or Peter of..." or "Peter the...." This was a pointer that in the kingdom of God the source of each believer's identity was to be God, with Jesus as elder brother.

John was to have a very similar experience. Not only was he to lose his identity as "the son of Zebedee, fisherman," but he was to be given a new identity as the sponsor of Jesus' mother, Mary (John 19:26–27).

People often fail to realize that, after Jesus' death and resurrection, the community generally did not know how to relate to those thousands of Jesus' followers who now had no blood household of identity. In the end the Romans referred to them contemptuously as "Christians"—belonging to the tribe of Christ. That name stuck, even though the Christians had called themselves "members of the Way of the Lord." Identity was what was applied by others, not by yourself. So "Christians" they became, and Christians they stayed.

PETER AND JOHN AS FISHERMEN

As Jesus passed along the Sea of Galilee, he saw Simon and his brother Andrew casting a net into the sea—for they were fishermen. And Jesus said to them, "Follow me and I will make you fish for people." And immediately they left their nets and followed him. As Jesus went a little farther, he saw James son of Zebedee and his brother John, who were in

their boat mending the nets. Immediately he called
them; and they left their father Zebedee in the boat
with the hired men, and followed him. (Mark 1:16–20)

Peter and John were canny sons of the rich entrepreneurs Jonah and Zebedee of Capernaum. These two men
jointly owned a fishing business that employed day
laborers in peak times. Fishing rights were jealously
guarded by the Roman authorities and used as a fertile
avenue for taxation. Fishing entrepreneurs bought fishing leases from government tax agents for a percentage
of the catch, often as high as 40 percent. They sold the
remaining catch either directly or through marketers.
Families of fishermen often formed partnerships in
order to minimize their tax and make their business
more efficient.

Fishing was done at night, using a long net that was let
down around a shoal of fish and then dragged into the
boat early in the morning, gathering the fish as it was
hauled in. After landing, the men would sort out the fish
in the presence of the tax inspector, agree on the amount
of tax and how it would be paid—in kind or coin—
organize the transport of the fish to the market, and then
repair and dry their nets for the next night's fishing.

Fishing entrepreneurs were hardheaded businessmen,
accustomed to haggling and dealing with all kinds of
people trying to force the price of their fish down. They
were used to competition from other fishermen and
from the larger fishing conglomerates who tried to
monopolize the fishing industry. In other words, they
were survivors in the cutthroat world of business.

They were also men of status in their village—at least
their fathers were, for it was the fathers who owned the
business. Zebedee and his partner Jonah were not poor;
they even employed laborers from their village. This

made them men of fairly high status. They were expected to make significant donations to their synagogue and to the temple at Jerusalem, and their names would be recorded each time such gifts were made. Family honor demanded that the eldest son take over the business when the father died. He would also take on other duties of honor, including caring for his mother and any of his parents' relatives still in the home, supervising the welfare of his younger brothers and helping them find suitable wives, and providing suitable husbands and dowries for any sisters. He would continue, too, the system of benefactions to his community.

Thus, when Peter and Andrew and James and John left home to follow Jesus, they walked away from their household responsibilities and brought shame upon their fathers. This was a part of the cost of their discipleship, a cost that would haunt them all their lives—especially when both fathers died soon afterward, their deaths probably hastened by this loss of honor in their community.

We need to move now into Jesus' last days in Jerusalem.

GALILEE AND JUDEA

First, a word about the relationships between Galilean and Judean Jews, because this is at the heart of the Gospel story. Galilee had been much more influenced by the Greek and Roman empires than had Judea. Galilean Jews generally spoke with a Greek accent and were thus easily recognized as soon as they opened their mouths. (This will come up later when we look at Peter's betrayal of Jesus.) They had learned to live comfortably with the Greeks and Romans in their area, which prompted the more conservative Judean Jews at Jerusalem to accuse the Galileans of not keeping strictly to the Mosaic law. A number of times, Pharisees from Jerusalem went into

Galilee to confront Jesus because they did not trust the
Galilean Pharisees to interpret the law correctly. Notice
John 7:49, in which the Jerusalem Pharisees accuse the
Galilean Jews of being accursed because they do not
know the law.

Jesus and all but one of his twelve disciples were from
Galilee. This is important, because these men were able
to relate more easily to non-Jews than were their Judean
counterparts. (The exception was Judas, as we will see
later.) The social dislocation of their calling to follow
Jesus, and their being Galileans, dogged them throughout their lives. Without understanding these two fac-
tors, we will never fully comprehend the dynamics of
Jesus' last days.

PETER

Peter was appointed by Jesus to be the leader of the
twelve. If Zebedee was the senior partner over Jonah in
the fishing partnership, then his older son, James, would
have been seen as the senior over Peter. In that case, the
appointing of Peter as the senior apostle would have
caused no little dissension among them. This may help
explain why, just before arriving in Jerusalem for Jesus'
last days, James and John take Jesus aside and ask that
they, and not Jonah's sons Peter and Andrew, become his
two senior men once the kingdom is established
(Matthew 20:20–28).

Peter was with the others when Jesus directed them to
the upper room to celebrate Passover, his last meal with
them, his beloved disciples.

All the gospels indicate that the room set aside for
Jesus and the twelve to celebrate Passover was a private
one, and that certain of the disciples were responsible for
preparing the room and the food. This meant that the

homeowner was not there to welcome them and conduct the usual rituals to deal with the dust on their feet and clothing. One of the twelve should have assumed that responsibility. With Jesus' words about what leadership implied still very much in their minds, Peter, at least, should have assumed the role of leader-as-slave.

The meal proceeded. Jesus kept dipping his unwashed hand into the food bowls as though he were not thereby making the food unfit for human consumption. The others then hesitatingly did the same and eventually they all acquiesced to this serious lack of normal order. But they were not really comfortable, and Jesus sensed it.

Not one of them had heeded Jesus' message about "whoever wishes to be first among you must be slave of all" (Mark 10:44) and taken on the task of serving the others. No doubt none of the twelve was prepared to do this shameful job because of his sense of honor. So Jesus left it to halfway through the meal to perform this slave service himself.

Jesus suddenly got up from the sofa on which he was reclining to eat, took off his outer robe, tied a towel around his waist, and filled a bowl with water. He then acted in the role of the household slave whose job it was to take off the dusty sandals of household members and guests, wash the dust from their feet, and then put slippers on them (John 13:4–5).

It is hard for us today to get inside the minds and hearts of these twelve men as their teacher and master and potential Messiah dishonored himself to the extent of disrobing in front of them. Remember, underclothing as we know it was not yet in use. There was a loose-fitting undergarment, but men did not normally doff their outer garments when at a formal meal. What Jesus was doing here was not only performing a task that strictly belonged to a slave, but he was dressed like any household slave would be when performing this task: no outer garment, only a towel wrapped around the waist over the loose undergarment.

In any case, these men were stunned into silence by Jesus' actions. Because this ritual was part of the welcoming ceremony, it should have been done before they entered the house. By doing it after they had entered and started eating, Jesus was taking the emphasis away from the out-of-placeness resulting from bringing dirt inside, and emphasizing instead the true role of leadership.

He knelt before each one—a gesture of respect to one of higher social status—took off the disciple's dusty sandals, took these to the door, maintaining a crouched position, and ritually shook the dust off outside the room, leaving the sandals there. He returned and dipped the disciple's feet, one at a time, into the water, wiping them with the towel around his waist and replacing the sandals with slippers from the pile inside the door. He stayed on his knees as he moved to the next disciple and repeated the ritual.

Notice, Jesus didn't begin with Peter. No doubt he wanted Peter to see him repeat this ritual several times in order to focus Peter's attention on the enormity of the situation. He wanted Peter to see what happens when leaders don't lead the kingdom way, forcing their Messiah to suffer the shame.

At last Jesus came on his knees to Peter. Peter's response is not easy to translate effectively into written English, because the Greek word order does not work in English. The nearest translation may be "Lord, *my* feet do you wash?"

To which Jesus responded with his hands on Peter's sandals, "What I am now doing you do not understand at this moment. But later on you will."

Peter was adamant. "*My* feet you will never, never wash."

Then the moment of truth: "Have it your own way, Peter. But, if I do not dip your feet in water right now, then I cannot own you as mine, ever."

Peter was dumbfounded! Here he was, like the other eleven disciples, without any household identity or honor whatsoever, either in their own eyes or in the eyes of the communities they had dishonored. But Peter, you see, was also somewhat ashamed because he should have done this job, having been appointed their leader. Peter was given by word and example a model of how a teacher should be: not one who dominates with a show of expertise, but one who empowers pupils. Peter struggled with this concept all his days, never really coming to terms with what being a leader in the kingdom actually involved.

Jesus returned to his place and broke the bread and shared the cup of wine as an acted parable of his coming redemptive, sacrificial death. Jesus told Peter plainly that Judas was not the only betrayer, but that Peter, too, would betray him.

After the meal, Peter was there when Jesus led the disciples out into the garden at Gethsemane and called upon him and James and John to pray with him. But they all fell asleep and let Jesus down just when he was in deep need of friendship and understanding.

Peter was there when the mob arrived under Judas' leadership to take Jesus captive. It was Peter who forgot all the warnings Jesus had given about this event and took out his sword to protect his master, cutting off the right ear of the high priest's slave, Malchus. And Peter was there, among the soldiers, trying to listen in on their plans for Jesus so he could mount a rescue. When challenged, he denied ever knowing Jesus (John 18:15–18; 25–27; Matthew 26:69–74).

Peter was *not* there when Jesus was crucified. Here we must remember Peter's social position. He had brought

dishonor upon his father's household by leaving home to
follow Jesus. In Galilee he was pilloried because of this.
He had no social position in the community at all. He
was a nobody, having no household with which to be
identified. He was *persona non grata*—a nameless individual with no status. But Peter had hoped that, when
Jesus came into his kingdom, he would be Jesus' senior
governor and have status and honor far above what he
had left behind.

Peter could not now even rejoin his kin household. He
had deserted his father and now his Lord and master,
Jesus. In spite of the three solid years of training and
teaching Jesus had given him, he was a failure. Did the
human Jesus feel he had made a tragic mistake in select-
ing Peter as leader?

JOHN

John was there when Peter denied ever knowing Jesus. It
had been John, with friends in the temple bureaucracy,
who had made it possible for them both to be in the
high priest's courtyard with the soldiers.

John, who with his older brother, James, sought to be
appointed Jesus' top officials when the kingdom finally
arrived, did not run away. He too heard the cock crow a
second time and remembered Jesus' warning to Peter. He
must have grieved for his friend.

It was John who returned and stood with Mary at the
foot of the cross (John 19:25–27). Mary had no male relatives left except her other sons, James, Joseph, Simon,
and Judas. But Jesus was not prepared to leave his mother
in their care since they had not believed in him. By leaving her in John's care, Jesus solved a twin problem: he
gave John an identity as his mother's sponsor, and he
gave his mother a new household with which she could
be identified and in which she could be cared for.

So, although John had fallen asleep along with James and Peter in Gethsemane when he should have been praying with Jesus, he partially redeemed himself by being the only apostle to stand beside Jesus at the cross and accept the responsibility of caring for Jesus' mother.

CONCLUSION

These two men, shamed in the eyes of their community for walking away from their fathers' households, and now having no identity—no household head as their name—were typical of the twelve. They were fallible but lovable men on whom Jesus depended, knowing that they would never be perfect. Jesus gave them both new identities, so great was his love for these two disciples, even though they had let him down so badly. When all the twelve were most needed, they were not there. In fact, all but one left Jesus to suffer alone.

DISCUSSION QUESTIONS

1. How does our commitment to Christ and our church impinge upon our personal identity?
2. What kinds of experiences tempt us to deny our commitment to Christ and his values?
3. How does "being there for Jesus" relate to our being there for others in dire need of support?

Mary Magdalene and Her Coworkers, and Martha and Mary

In Mediterranean society in Jesus day, women had no identity as women. They were known only in relationship to men. A woman was "the daughter of…," "the wife of…," "the mother of…," "the niece of…," "the granddaughter of…," "the daughter-in-law of…"; otherwise, she did not exist. Even women in the highest orders of society were identified in relationship to a dominant male. A woman never gave identity to a male.

As a result, single, unattached women—widows with no male sponsor, orphaned daughters with no brothers or other male sponsors—were an embarrassment to ancient society generally. When Jesus came across the funeral of the only son of the widow of Nain, he brought her son back to life for her sake, not the son's, so that she would have a male sponsor to give her an identity and care for her (Luke 7:11–17).

If female members of a household earned money by taking in washing or doing housework, they could not receive the money into their own hands: the head of the household had to be paid directly. The only way any woman could earn money directly was through prostitution. Because there were no social organizations to care

for single, unattached women, the very first charitable work
the early church undertook was the care of widows—
finding households in which to embed them and give them
an identity, as well as providing them with living expenses.

Remember the story of Dorcas at Joppa, a single
woman who herself was probably a widow with money
left her by her husband (Acts 9:36–42)? She set up her
household as a hospice for householdless widows and
cared for them. When she died suddenly, the men in her
community begged Peter to come and bring her back to
life, no doubt to save them the responsibility of looking
after all those pesky and demanding widows! This he was
happy to do, especially as he had been part of the decision to look after widows in Jerusalem. When you read
about widows in Paul's letter to Timothy, remember that
there would inevitably have been some families who
were unwilling to take care of younger widows and
therefore passed them over to the Christian congrega-
tions (1 Timothy 5:3–16).

What set Jesus and the early church apart was that
women were addressed directly and not through their
household head, and that they were named in their own
right and not necessarily in relation to a male sponsor. In
fact, unless a married couple was being referred to, Paul
always addressed women by their own names, a remark-
able case of breaking a deep social taboo.

OUT-OF-PLACENESS

Another core value of Mediterranean society that is cen-
tral to any understanding of the people of the New
Testament is the concept of being "out-of-place." All per-
sons, animals and things were given their proper place in
the household and community. When anything moved
out of its place, rituals had to be invoked to restore order.

The term "unclean" was not a hygienic description but a spatial one: "unclean" really meant "causing social disorder." When everyone and everything was in the proper place, then there was peace; and peace was not about an inner emotional feeling but about good order.

Dirt too, was an example of out-of-placeness. In its proper place outside the house, on the roads, in the fields, dirt posed no threats to social order. Indeed, dirt was needed if crops were to grow and people and farm animals fed. But when dirt entered the house by whatever means, it was out of its proper place and had to be dealt with immediately. This had nothing to do with any notions of hygiene or personal cleanliness. The dirt simply should not be there because its place was outside the house. Because this was a social problem, the out-of-place dirt had to be dealt with publicly so that everyone would know that order had been restored. Part of the welcome ritual, then, was that family members and guests, before entering the house, had their sandals removed and placed outside the door, their bare feet dipped in water and wiped with a towel, and a pair of slippers placed on their feet. In richer households, an outer garment was draped around the guests to prevent dust on the clothes dropping off inside. This ritual was always performed by the lowest-status member of the household—by a household slave if one was owned.

A group of items that always caused disorder when out of place was whatever emerged from orifices of the human body. Again, this had nothing to do with cleanliness. While inside the body, blood, for example, was in its right place and therefore no cause for concern. But when it emerged because of an injury, a sickness, or a natural phenomenon like childbirth, the blood was out of place and had to be dealt with by some public ritual.

A very good example of this was Jesus' healing of the
woman with a running sore (Matthew 9:18–26; Mark
5:21–43; Luke 8:40–56). When this woman had brushed
past many people to get to Jesus, touching their clothing,
she had made them out of place in the process and created
wholesale disorder. As she was healed, Jesus said to her,
"Go in peace." He thus not only restored her to an orderly
life with her family, but he also restored order to the
whole crowd following him, and they knew it. They were
no longer out of place because of being touched by her.

In the case of childbirth, the mother was not allowed to
associate socially with anyone else for a certain period—
it varied with the sex of the baby—and then had to
attend a ceremony at the temple or synagogue to signal
her return to her rightful place. In the case of injury, the
victim had to bathe and put on another set of clothes
before returning to social contact with others. During
the period of out-of-placeness, should the victim inad-
vertently touch the clothes of another person, then that
person, too, was declared to be out of place and had to
bathe and reclothe before resuming social contacts.

Social relations were very much dependent upon
everyone and everything being in their proper place. A
great deal of the Gospel narrative makes no sense to us
today because we have fundamentally different ways of
relating to each other and our physical environment.

MARY MAGDALENE AND HER COWORKERS

> Soon afterwards [Jesus] went on through cities and
> villages [of Galilee], proclaiming and bringing the
> good news of the kingdom of God. The twelve were
> with him, as well as some women who had been
> cured of evil spirits and infirmities: Mary, called
> Magdalene, from whom seven demons had gone out,

and Joanna, the wife of Herod's steward Chuza, and
Susanna, and many others, who provided for them
out of their resources. (Luke 8:1–3)

We first meet Mary of Magdala in the list of women
who, out of gratitude for the healing that Jesus had
brought them, banded together to help Jesus and his
twelve disciples by arranging food and accommodation
as they traveled around Galilee. This was no easy task,
since it required them to abandon their domestic duties
for days at a time and even risk bringing shame on their
respective household heads by traveling without male
chaperons.

In an open society, everyone had to know why travel
outside the village was necessary and what the ultimate
destination was; otherwise, the household head would be
shamed and the community would be in disorder. We
read of Jesus and his disciples traveling all around
Galilee. We see Paul, too, going all around the
Mediterranean world, and we don't stop to think what
this involved. You will notice, for instance, that Luke
often indicates where Paul stayed during a journey. This
was important to his readers, since the last thing Paul
wanted was to cause disorder as a stranger.

The band of women that traveled around Galilee helping Jesus and the disciples included Mary of Magdala,
Joanna the wife of Chuza, Herod's steward, and Susanna.
Finding food and accommodation for thirteen homeless
men who had given up their identity by deserting their
households was no easy matter. Throughout Galilee
there were few inns, but, as inns were places of ill-repute
patronized mostly by highway robbers and dishonest
merchants, it is unlikely that Jesus and his men stayed in
any of them anyway. This meant that these women
would have had to trade on their own networks of family

households and do a great deal of cajoling to make sure
that Jesus and his followers had a pillow at night and sufficient food to keep them going during the day. The men,
of course, had given up their own means of earning a living, so they had to rely entirely upon these women for
their basic sustenance.

Mary of Magdala (from the village of Magdala) was
certainly the most well known female figure to follow
Jesus. That she is not named in connection with a male
sponsor could mean that she was single. This may have
led to the myth that she was a prostitute, as prostitution was the only way independent women could earn
a living; however, there is not a hint of this in the
Gospels nor in any of the postapostolic literature.
Mary is listed first, indicating that she was most probably the leading woman in this band and coordinated all
their work. This makes her a good organizer and a
hardheaded businesswoman—not unlike Jesus' twelve
male disciples.

When Jesus arrived in Jerusalem for those final days,
there was nothing these women could do to help. As
Galileans, they would have had few networks of friends
or family in Judea. Even Joanna, wife of Herod's steward,
would have found it difficult to exert any influence at all,
since the Judean temple bureaucracy was so opposed to
Jesus.

But it is clear that at least Mary Magdalene, Joanna,
and Susanna stayed with Jesus during this time. They
stood watching his crucifixion from afar, followed Joseph
of Arimathea to the tomb, and then returned after the
Sabbath in order to finish the work of embalming their
Lord's body.

They were the first to see Jesus alive after his resurrection, and they were given a message to pass on to the disciples. But those eleven men, even after all the women
had done for them over the past three years, still treated

their words with contempt (Luke 24:10–11). We need to
remember that in a Jewish law court, any woman's evidence had to be corroborated by at least two credible
male witnesses. Without male witnesses, the disciples
were unprepared to listen to the women.

After the disciples went to see the empty tomb for
themselves, they returned home. But Mary of Magdala
remained and was given a special visitation by Jesus.

> But Mary stood weeping outside the tomb. As she
> wept, she bent over to look into the tomb; and she
> saw two angels in white, sitting where the body of
> Jesus had been lying, one at the head and the other
> at the feet. They said to her, "Woman, why are you
> weeping?" She said to them, "They have taken away
> my Lord, and I do not know where they have laid
> him." When she had said this, she turned around and
> saw Jesus standing there, but she did not know that
> it was Jesus. Jesus said to her, "Woman, why are you
> weeping? Whom are you looking for?" Supposing
> him to be the gardener, she said to him, "Sir, if you
> have carried him away, tell me where you have laid
> him, and I will take him away." Jesus said to her,
> "Mary!" She turned and said to him in Hebrew,
> "Rabbouni!" (which means Teacher). Jesus said to
> her, "Do not hold on to me, because I have not yet
> ascended to the Father. But go to my brothers and
> say to them, 'I am ascending to my Father and your
> Father, to my God and your God.'" Mary Magdalene
> went and announced to the disciples, "I have seen
> the Lord"; and she told them that he had said these
> things to her. (John 20:11–18)

What we see in all these women was loyalty and
devotion to Jesus. They were there with him every step
of the way.

MARTHA AND MARY

It is very interesting to notice how John introduces
Martha and Mary: "Now a certain man was ill, Lazarus
of Bethany, the village of Mary and her sister Martha"
(John 11:1). This is curious, since Lazarus was the head
of that household, and was, by the time of writing, well
known as the one whom Jesus had raised from the dead.
This means that these two sisters had become well
respected as special friends of Jesus in their own right.

Luke introduces these two sisters as being at home on
their own when Jesus decided to pay them a visit.

> Now as they went on their way, he entered a certain
> village, where a woman named Martha welcomed
> him into her home. She had a sister named Mary,
> who sat at the Lord's feet and listened to what he was
> saying. But Martha was distracted by her many tasks;
> so she came to him and asked, "Lord, do you not
> care that my sister has left me to do all the work by
> myself? Tell her then to help me." But the Lord
> answered her, "Martha, Martha, you are worried and
> distracted by many things; there is need of only one
> thing. Mary has chosen the better part, which will
> not be taken away from her." (Luke 10:38–42)

So, there Jesus was, a Jewish man on his own in a
house with two Jewish women, something expressly for-
bidden by Jewish social conventions. The Jewish
Mishnah gives this direction:

A. A man should not remain alone with two women, but
   a woman may remain alone with two men.
B. R. Simeon says, "Also: One may stay alone with two
   women, when his wife is with him.

C. "And he sleeps with them in the same inn,
D. "because his wife keeps watch over him" (Mishnah
    Qiddushin 4:12).

The whole village would end up walking by to see
whether anything inappropriate was going on. This was
an open society, so that doors and windows were thrown
open to public view during the day. Closed doors and
windows meant there was something to hide.

In this story, Martha's concern was for their reputation. Both sisters should have been on their feet and
moving around so that the villagers could see they were
behaving correctly. (Actually, Martha, as the senior of the
two, should have asked Jesus not to enter, but to return
when Lazarus was there.) Mary, however, wanted to sit
on the floor at Jesus' feet and listen to him. She needed
to give Jesus all her attention and concentrate in order to
learn, whereas Martha was the one who could work and
listen at the same time.

Jesus understood Martha's concern for the social
niceties and gently rebuked her. Jesus was not making a
distinction between the practical Martha and the spiritual Mary. Martha, as the senior sister, was concerned for
maintaining their social standing and moral rectitude in
a society where women were expected to make sure the
honor of their menfolk was maintained. In this case both
her brother Lazarus and her guest Jesus risked being
shamed, so it was her duty, and not Jesus', either to ask
him to leave or to make sure that both sisters stayed on
their feet and kept moving so that the village could not
accuse them of doing anything untoward.

It is interesting that later, when Jesus returned to raise
Lazarus from the dead, Martha was the one who showed
greater understanding of Jesus' teaching than did her sister. Mary greeted Jesus with "Lord, if you had been here,

my brother would not have died." Martha said the same
thing but added, "But even now I know that God will
give you whatever you ask of him" (John 11:22). She had
also responded to Jesus' question with, "I know that
[Lazarus] will rise again in the resurrection on the last
day." (See the whole account in John 11:1–44.) And, of
course, Jesus raised Lazarus so that he could continue to
provide for his sisters, rather than allow them to become
prostitutes in order to survive.

Later on, Lazarus invited Jesus to his house for a meal.
We need to remember here that John did not write
chronologically but wove his story thematically, so that,
although this incident occurs early in the Gospel, it was
in fact a part of Jesus' last days on earth.

> Six days before the Passover Jesus came to Bethany, the
> home of Lazarus, whom he had raised from the dead.
> There they gave a dinner for him. Martha served, and
> Lazarus was one of those at the table with him. Mary
> took a pound of costly perfume made of pure nard,
> anointed Jesus' feet, and wiped them with her hair.
> The house was filled with the fragrance of the per-
> fume. But Judas Iscariot, one of his disciples (the one
> who was about to betray him), said, "Why was this
> perfume not sold for three hundred denarii and the
> money given to the poor?" (He said this not because
> he cared about the poor, but because he was a thief;
> he kept the common purse and used to steal what
> was put into it.) Jesus said, "Leave her alone. She
> bought it so that she might keep it for the day of my
> burial. You always have the poor with you, but you do
> not always have me." (John 12:1–8)

There were fourteen men at the dinner at Lazarus'
home, and the two sisters remained in the kitchen, with

Martha, the senior sister, serving the food. Mary came
out with an alabaster jar of precious Indian nard, worth
a workman's whole year's wages. To appreciate this gesture we will need to understand another core value.

A World of Limited Good

Everything, Mediterraneans believed, including honor
and goodness, was in limited supply. Whereas we can
save up and buy whatever we want, and often wait until
something comes onto the supermarket shelves,
Mediterraneans held that what you had was what you
were born with and the only way you could accumulate
extra was to steal from others. If a sheep farmer suddenly
had an additional sheep or goat, his neighbors would
have immediately suspected that he stole it. This was
how Mediterraneans processed their world, and we must
bear this in mind when reading about charity and giving
to the poor and needy.

The benefaction system was one in which money and
service were exchanged, always to the benefit of the rich.
The only way people became rich was by stealing from
the poor through oppression and manipulation of working conditions. This is why the New Testament is so full
of condemnation of the rich and the Old Testament
prophets so full of concern for the poor and powerless.

It is hard for us today to comprehend this notion that
there is a limited stockpile of everything, including
moral imperatives. What was in each person's world was
all there was to go around. To try to acquire more than
his status entitled him to was to act shamefully. The
term "rich" in the Bible always refers to those who have
acquired more than their due; "poor" refers to those
who, by misfortune or theft, have had their share of the
pile reduced.

This jar of nard was probably Mary's dowry, given to
her by her father, and protected by her brother Lazarus.
Although she owned it, she had no right to spend it;
once it was used up, it was gone and could not be
replaced. The dowry was handed on by the household
head to the bridegroom, who was duty-bound to keep it
as part of his household assets. This was why dowries
were invariably goods and not money.

Now, when Mary came into the dining room, broke
open her dowry of precious nard, anointed Jesus' head
and feet with the ointment, and spread it evenly with her
hair, in the eyes of all present she was misusing and wast-
ing her dowry. Judas moaned about the waste of goods
and how the poor could have been helped, when in fact
he couldn't have cared less for any of the poor. Mary
could never replace this dowry, except by stealing from
her sister Martha's dowry—something Mary would
never have contemplated.

Mary had not used all the ointment. But Jesus, who
didn't care at all about what the others thought of her
gesture, said she should keep what was left and use that
for embalming him after his death. No doubt Mary and
Martha were there that resurrection morning, among the
women who gathered to go to the tomb and complete
the task of embalming their precious Lord's body. But
Jesus was not there, so Mary was left with only half her
dowry, unable to do as Jesus had suggested.

In Martha and Mary Jesus had two loyal and dedicated women who remained committed to him to the
bitter end. They may not have fully understood why
their Lord and master had to die and rise again, but they
entrusted themselves to him, even risking the shame
that their actions may have brought on their brother
and their village.

CONCLUSION

Thus, women played a crucial role during Jesus' mission. Some traveled ahead and organized food and accommodation, thus putting their menfolk at risk of being shamed in the eyes of their community. Others were prepared to challenge the mores of their society to express their devotion to Jesus. These same women were there to weep at his cross and to be the first recipients of the good news that Jesus had arisen from the grave. These women demonstrated the very kind of kingdom leadership that Jesus had demanded of his twelve male disciples, even though they had not been there to hear Jesus actually describe that leadership.

DISCUSSION QUESTIONS

1. How do social expectations affect the practical application of our commitment to Christ?
2. What examples have you had in your own life in which practical, behind-the-scenes work for your church has been undervalued? Have you unwittingly undervalued others in the same way?
3. To what extent is your expectation of being recognized for the work you do for Christ and the church a factor in deciding whether or not to volunteer for such work?

HER⊙D, PİLATE, CAİAPHAS, AND JUDAS ⊙F KERİ⊙TH

We move now from some of Jesus' disciples and friends to a few political and religious leaders whom Jesus succeeded in offending and turning against him. Their attitudes toward him and his disciples proved crucial in bringing about his final demise. In addition, we'll look at the one disciple who was not a Galilean—Judas of Kerioth—but who decided to ally himself with the authorities who were bent on Jesus' downfall.

To understand why they came to treat Jesus as an enemy, we need to consider the way both the political and religious authorities saw themselves and their authority.

HER⊙D ANTİPAS

In the middle of the first century B.C., when Palestine came under the total domination of the Roman Empire, Herod the Great became the first appointed governor of the region. He was, in many ways, a typical ruler of his day and did much to alienate the Jews he governed. Herod was the one who was unsettled by the Magi's coming in search of the newborn king of the Jews. He was, after all, the present king of the Jews; he had enough trouble fighting off other members of his family who wanted his throne. Before he died he executed his own son Antipater, leaving Antipas, a son by a Samaritan woman, as his heir.

Antipas became tetrarch of Galilee and Perea, while his older brother, Archelaus, assumed their father's rule over the rest of the Middle Eastern area. They were never at peace with each other, fighting over their father's will to the bitter end. A half-brother, Philip, had a much smaller area under his control.

Antipas married a Nabatean princess on orders from his father Herod the Great. This was a purely political alliance, designed to keep the Jews in order. But, on a journey to Rome, Antipas visited his half-brother Philip and became enamored of Philip's wife Herodias, who was also Antipas' niece. She ended up divorcing Philip. When Antipas' wife learned of this, she fled back to her father Aretas and divorced Antipas. This left the conspirators free and they married quietly. Herodias thus ascended to the position of the wife of the tetrarch of Galilee and Perea. She brought with her the lusty Salome, her daughter by Philip.

John the Baptizer accused Antipas and Herodias of doubly breaking the Jewish law—for Antipas had married the divorced wife of a man who was still alive and who had a living child. Herodias never forgave him for exposing her to the general public; she was determined to have his head. This she eventually did, and it was one of the many disgraces of the reign of Antipas.

> Herod had arrested John, bound him, and put him in prison on account of Herodias, his brother Philip's wife, because John had been telling him, "It is not lawful for you to have her." Though Herod wanted to put him to death, he feared the crowd, because they regarded him as a prophet. But when Herod's birthday came, the daughter of Herodias danced before the company, and she pleased Herod so much that he promised on oath to grant her

whatever she might ask. Prompted by her mother, she said, "Give me the head of John the Baptist here on a platter." The king was grieved, yet out of regard for his oaths and for his guests, he commanded it to be given; he sent and had John beheaded in the prison. The head was brought on a platter and given to the girl, who brought it to her mother. (Matthew 14:3–11)

Before his final trial in front of Antipas, Jesus had encountered Antipas twice before. Early on, just after the Baptizer had been beheaded, when news of Jesus' activities reached him, Antipas sent officials out to have Jesus brought to him for questioning, to make sure that Jesus was not the Baptizer resurrected (Matthew 14:1–2; Mark 6:14–16; Luke 9:7–9). Clearly, Antipas was suspicious of Jesus, but decided not to use force to bring him in for fear of starting up another insurrection among the Jews, who at that stage were clearly applauding Jesus. In the meantime, Jesus left Antipas' territory to pursue his mission elsewhere.

The next time Jesus encountered Antipas was when Jesus entered Jerusalem for the last time. By now Antipas had heard enough to make him sure that Jesus was a threat and must be stopped. The Baptizer had succeeded in ruining Antipas' reputation, and now this Jesus was stirring up the Jews to such an extent that Antipas couldn't be sure of maintaining peace in the land. He let it be known that he had taken steps to have Jesus murdered.

When Jesus was told by some apparently sympathetic Pharisees that Antipas was after him, he sent the Pharisees off to Antipas with a word that must have really put him in a rage. "Go and tell that fox for me that nothing will get in the way of my mission. When I am murdered, it will be right here in Jerusalem for all to see" (see Luke 13: 32–35). In other words, Jesus saw this as a

ploy to get him out of the city so that Antipas' minions
could secretly dispose of him without anyone suspecting
who was really behind it. But there would be no hidden
assassination: Jesus would be executed by powers clearly
visible to all; and these powers would have to answer to
God and to the people for their heinous crime.

IN-GROUP AND OUT-GROUP

This core value of Mediterranean society of biblical times
is essential for any understanding of how Jews related to
each other and to the outside world. The only two groups
of people were the in-group and the out-group—in our
terms, "them" and "us," although even within "us" there
could be some members of an out-group.

An example of this division was the strong differences
between the Pharisees and the Herodians. The Pharisees
began as groups of men committed to the Mosaic law
and its ongoing traditions. They were the fundamental-
ists of their day and hated the aristocracy who played fast
and loose with the Scriptures. In particular, they hated
the Herodians, members of the family of Herod the
Great, who formed a clan of high-status power and
wealth in Jerusalem. No Herodians had friends who were
Pharisees, and no Pharisees had friends who were
Herodians. There was a clear line between them, an
invisible barrier of class and theology that kept them
apart. But, as both Matthew and Mark report, they came
together over one man: Jesus. He was "out" to both
groups, so they combined forces to try to get rid of him
(Matthew 22:16; Mark 3:6; 12:13).

Society generally drew the boundaries based on social
status and attitudes, but Jesus drew his boundaries based
on obedience to the Gospel. It is important to keep this
aspect of division in Mediterranean society well to the

fore when trying to understand the dynamics behind the Gospel stories. Judeans and Galileans never resolved their differences, any more than did Jews and Samaritans. So why did the Pharisees, who hated Jesus so much, warn him about Herod's plot to kill him? Well, Jesus was a fellow Israelite and therefore, as far as the Herodians were concerned, part of their "out-group." The Pharisees did not want the Herodians to have any say in what happened to Jesus. If Jesus was to be dealt with, the Pharisees wanted to do it themselves. So, they warned Jesus of the plot to murder him, no doubt hoping he would flee from the city and leave them able to deal with him themselves. But Jesus was no coward. He sent them off with a message to Herod, calling him a fox—a low and cunning animal that had no courage whatsoever.

Finally, Jesus was captured and eventually taken before Herod Antipas.

> When Herod saw Jesus, he was very glad, for he had been wanting to see him for a long time, because he had heard about him and was hoping to see him perform some sign. He questioned him at some length, but Jesus gave him no answer. The chief priests and the scribes stood by, vehemently accusing him. Even Herod with his soldiers treated him with contempt and mocked him; then he put an elegant robe on him and sent him back to Pilate. That same day Herod and Pilate became friends with each other; before this they had been enemies. (Luke 23:8–12)

Antipas was delighted that Pilate, procurator of Judea, had sent Jesus to him because Jesus was a Galilean by birth. He was determined to make the most of this occasion. He tried to get Jesus to do some magic tricks, no doubt so that his own conjurers could show him up as a fake. But Jesus said and did nothing. He gave Antipas not one moment's satisfaction. So Antipas dressed him up in royal purple and sent him back to Pilate under a royal escort with a word of thanks to his fellow administrator. From that day on they forgot their jealousy and became the best of friends.

Herod Antipas was typical of the Roman governors who espoused self-glory and gratification, making names for themselves by building monuments and cities to themselves and their emperors. They tolerated no criticism and punished every person who did not bow his knee and obey their every wish. Jesus, who did not show much attention to basic social conventions, refused to bend to such political leaders. Although not leading a political revolution, he nevertheless encouraged civil disobedience in his followers, and thus was a threat.

PONTIUS PILATE

When Jesus came into Judea, he brought himself within the jurisdiction of a rather different political leader, Pontius Pilate. Whereas Antipas had some Jewish blood in him and knew Judaism from the inside, Pilate was a Roman and an outsider to the Jews.

Pilate was a rich Italian with sufficient money and assets to ensure a succession of government appointments. He was made procurator of Palestine in A.D. 26, just a few years before Jesus' crucifixion. His position was that of immediate military and judicial oversight of his area, reporting directly to the governor of Syria. Pilate had no sympathy at all toward the Jews and tried hard to bring them into line with the official Roman policy on foreigners. He was brutal in his administration. He showed his contempt toward the Jews when he appropriated the corban temple trust moneys to build an aqueduct some thirty kilometers long to bring water into the city.

Pilate had no inhibitions at all about killing Jews who showed signs of resisting his policies. The atrocity mentioned in Luke 13:1–2 was typical. Because only Pilate had the power to authorize execution, the Jews had to seek his approval for any capital punishment they needed to mete out. (We should remember here that the later execution of Stephen by the Jews was illegal, but Pilate by then was loath to bring them to court over it.) On one occasion Pilate sent soldiers into the city carrying shields on which pagan emblems had been painted, with orders to erect a memorial to Caesar in the temple. The Jews simply laid down in front of the temple, prepared to be massacred to protect their beloved temple from pagan symbols. Pilate had to back down, and that hardly endeared the Jews to him.

When Jesus was brought before him in order to ratify the Sanhedrin's judgment of execution, he deliberately provoked them by deciding to try Jesus himself. In most cases he would have rubber-stamped their decisions, so why did he decide to retry Jesus himself? What did Pilate really think about Jesus? We will never know. Pilate simply used Jesus as a way of getting back at the Jews he hated and despised so much.

> Then Pilate took Jesus and had him flogged. And the soldiers wove a crown of thorns and put it on his head, and they dressed him in a purple robe. They kept coming up to him, saying, "Hail, King of the Jews!" and striking him on the face. Pilate went out again and said to them, "Look, I am bringing him out to you to let you know that I find no case against him." So Jesus came out, wearing the crown of thorns and the purple robe. Pilate said to them, "Here is the man!" When the chief priests and the police saw him, they shouted, "Crucify him! Crucify him!" Pilate said to them, "Take him yourselves and

crucify him; I find no case against him." The Jews
answered him, "We have a law, and according to that
law he ought to die because he has claimed to be the
Son of God."

Now when Pilate heard this, he was more afraid
than ever. He entered his headquarters again and
asked Jesus, "Where are you from?" But Jesus gave
him no answer. Pilate therefore said to him, "Do you
refuse to speak to me? Do you not know that I have
power to release you, and power to crucify you?"
Jesus answered him, "You would have no power over
me unless it had been given you from above; therefore the one who handed me over to you is guilty of
a greater sin." From then on Pilate tried to release
him, but the Jews cried out, "If you release this man,
you are no friend of the emperor. Everyone who
claims to be a king sets himself against the emperor."
When Pilate heard these words, he brought Jesus
outside and sat on the judge's bench at a place called
The Stone Pavement, or in Hebrew Gabbatha. Now
it was the day of the Preparation for the Passover;
and it was about noon. He said to the Jews, "Here is
your king!" They cried out, "Away with him! Away
with him! Crucify him!" Pilate asked them, "Shall I
crucify your King?" The chief priests answered, "We
have no king but the emperor." Then he handed him
over to them to be crucified. (John 19:1–16)

In the end, Pilate was no match for these masters of
political intrigue. The chief priests threatened to report
him to Caesar for siding with an anti-Roman revolution-
ary who arrogated the title "King of the Jews."

Jesus could easily have let Pilate off the hook simply
by establishing that he was not at all interested in poli-
tics or an earthly kingdom. He could have proved that

the problem was just a religious one between him and
the temple bureaucracy. But Jesus refused to play their
games and instead let both sides condemn themselves
and each other.

CAİAPHAS

One result of the Roman takeover of Israel was that the
local civil authority had the right to appoint the high
priest. This ensured that Rome maintained religious as
well as political control over the Jews.

Losing the right to appoint their own high priest was a
very bitter pill for the Jews to swallow, and that, taken
with the requirement to use Roman coins for everyday
trading, meant that the temple establishment was always
very anti-Rome. The emperors did give certain rights to
the Jews, rights that were not given to any of their other
colonists. Among these was the right to mint their own
money because of the Jewish objection to human images
on anything that entered the temple sanctuary.

Annas was appointed high priest in A.D. 6. He was then
deposed in favor of his five sons, who served until A.D.
18, when his son-in-law Caiaphas was appointed.
Caiaphas in turn was deposed in A.D. 36, not long after
Jesus' crucifixion. However, Annas continued to exercise
a great deal of influence within the religious establishment, so much so that the authorities took Jesus to him
first, before taking him to Caiaphas for the official trial
(John 18:13–24).

Jesus refused to answer Annas' questions, simply
referring to the fact that he had taught openly in the
temple and that any of the worshippers could tell Annas
what he had taught. John does not report the interroga-
tion that took place in the house of Caiaphas. The other
Gospels indicate that he was brought before the official

assembly and that he refused to answer their questions directly. He foretold their future destruction, rather than his own.

Caiaphas urged the council to have Jesus murdered. As John reports it, the chief priests were concerned about the raising of Lazarus and the effect it had in promoting Jesus throughout Judea. They referred to the "many signs" that he was performing, which would lead the whole city to believe in him as Messiah. That would bring Roman intervention and much bloodshed.

Caiaphas then accused the chief priests of being idiots.

> Many of the Jews therefore, who had come with Mary [sister of Lazarus] and had seen what Jesus did [in raising Lazarus from the dead], believed in him. But some of them went to the Pharisees and told them what he had done. So the chief priests and the Pharisees called a meeting of the council, and said, "What are we to do? This man is performing many signs. If we let him go on like this, everyone will believe in him, and the Romans will come and destroy both our holy place and our nation." But one of them, Caiaphas, who was high priest that year, said to them, "You know nothing at all! You do not understand that it is better for you to have one man die for the people than to have the whole nation destroyed." He did not say this on his own, but being high priest that year he prophesied that Jesus was about to die for the nation, and not for the nation only, but to gather into one the dispersed people of God. So from that day on they planned to put him to death. (John 11:45–53)

Because Jesus did not appear first at the temple and announce his Messiahship to the religious leadership, he was branded as a traitor to Israel. That he announced himself first to Galileans was bad enough, but that he constantly denounced the temple leaders as hypocrites and self-servers was too much. Nothing that Jesus could have said or done—after he arrived in Jerusalem to the welcome hosannas of the peasants and farmers—could have saved him from being executed.

Caiaphas had to play a double game. He was appointed by Rome and therefore had to protect himself if he was to stay in office. Rome made it very clear what it expected of its minions. But Caiaphas also had to appease the masses who had seen in Jesus a new kind of Messiah, one who did not arrogate the trappings of office. Caiaphas' plan was to make it appear as though the Roman authorities, in the person of Pilate, had condemned Jesus to death.

As with the civil authorities, Jesus refused to take part in their games. He knew what the future was, and he let the present take care of itself. It is interesting that nowhere in the New Testament is there any evidence of Jesus or his followers taking part, or exhorting others to take part, in any political uprising or dissent. If anyone had a right to fight openly against political and religious oppression, it was Jesus. Obviously, he had a different way of dealing with human religious and political life.

JUDAS OF KERİOTH

Judas was the only Judean among Jesus' twelve disciples. It was inevitable, in a way, that he would be the disaffected one among them, given the "us" and "them" relationship between the Judean and Galilean Jews.

In their descriptions of Judas, the Gospels vary from betrayer to robber of the common purse. We are never really told why Judas betrayed Jesus. All we can do is try to understand him as much as is possible. One way to do

this is to imagine what Judas might say for himself on
the charge of being the betrayer of Jesus. Perhaps he
would answer something like the following:

Betrayer? Betrayer! Why do you keep calling me
betrayer? It wasn't me who betrayed Jesus, it was all
those other wimps from Galilee! Yes, wimps! That's
what they all were—wimps. Even Jesus! The only
time any of them showed any guts was when we
were all in Samaria that time, and the elders of a
Samaritan village told us all to clear out and not
come near the place, so James and John wanted to
burn down the village. But Jesus the wimp, of
course, stopped them.

What is it with those Galileans? The trouble is
they've lived too close for too long with all those
Greeks and Romans—dirty rotten Gentiles, all of
them! The Galilean Jews have had it too easy.
They've learned to accept the Greek and Roman
overlords and have given up our sacred mission to
free ourselves from them. We Jews should never be
slaves to any nation! We are God's own nation and
should never stop fighting for our rightful freedom.

You see, I was the only non-Galilean Jew among
Jesus' twelve disciples. I had wangled myself into
being the treasurer. You know who they really wanted
as treasurer? Matthew! Matthew, the tax collector!
The tax collectors for the Roman overlords were all
Galileans. Tax collectors were given a license to gath-
er taxes from us Jews and keep a hefty portion for
themselves before passing the rest on to the Roman
government. We hated them, Galilean traitors! Jews
should never give taxes to any other nation.

I persuaded the others that Matthew had proved
he was a tax fiddler and so could not be trusted with

our money. So, once I got control of our common purse, I started salting funds away for the future, when I would be the first king of free Israel. We had several rich women in our team, so we never wanted for food and accommodation. Soon I had a tidy sum stashed away for my future palace.

I'll tell you what my plan was. As soon as Jesus became popular with the people, not only in Galilee but also in Jerusalem, I would go to the high priests Annas and Caiaphas. I knew them personally. They were power-hungry and rich. They weren't wimps either—they would send off their temple police to put down a riot at the drop of a mitre. I would persuade them to support Jesus as Messiah.

Once Jesus had established Israel as an independent kingdom again, he would be allowed to reign for a few months. Then he would be paid off to retire early, maybe marry Mary Magdalene and settle down somewhere in his beloved Galilee and raise children and live to a happy and prosperous old age. Then I would take over as King of Israel and make the temple priests and their bureaucracy my senate—the actual governing body of the state. I just wanted position and riches and fame—they could have the real power and the responsibility of running the state.

Well, everything was going according to plan. After three years of careful planning, Jesus was led in triumph into Jerusalem on that stupid donkey. And the whole countryside came out to welcome their new king. "Hosanna!" they shouted. "Blessed is he who comes in the name of the Lord Yahweh!" they shouted. Poor fools.

The time was ripe for my next move. I went off to the high priests. They were really angry with Jesus. They saw him as a threat to their power and authority over the people. Jesus had being saying stupid things about the priests and the Pharisees, about all the temple bureaucracy. I tried to stop him from being so outspoken, but he wouldn't listen.

The priests were very interested in my plan. I persuaded them that Jesus' invective against them was a ploy to gain the support of the people. The people, you see, really hated the temple authorities. I persuaded the priests that it was in their own best interest to support Jesus as a coup leader. Jesus was the one who had popular support and would succeed in any uprising against Rome.

Then I told them about my plan to replace Jesus once he had been king for a few months and how I would give them the actual governing power in return for my purely ceremonial position as king. They seemed overcome with joy and elation at my plan. They promised their complete cooperation. They even gave me thirty pieces of silver as a deposit on my future palace! Do you know how much that was? One hundred twenty denarii—120 days' wages for a laborer. Not much—the rotten misers. But it was proof that they were with me—or so I thought.

So I waited for the time when Jesus would proclaim himself king.

Then it happened. Jesus ordered us to prepare for the Passover. That would be the time, I realized. After we celebrated the release of the Jews from Egyptian captivity several hundred years ago, Jesus would then announce our release from the captivity of Rome. I went quietly off to the priests and alerted them. The idea was that they would send their temple guard to join in Jesus' triumphal march to the temple. The priests would then help crown Jesus king of Jerusalem!

After the Passover meal, Jesus led us to his special place—the place I knew would be where he would begin his triumphant march—the garden of Gethsemane. When the time came, I gave the signal. I kissed Jesus twice on the cheek. This was so that the Jewish guards, hidden in the olive trees, would know which one was Jesus. He dressed like an ordinary man, you see, and it would have been difficult to distinguish him from the rest of us.

The guards rushed out of hiding and took hold of Jesus. They were supposed to carry him on their shoulders to the temple and announce the new kingdom of Israel. Instead, they bound his hands and hobbled his feet and took him prisoner, like a common criminal. I shouted to them to stop. By this time the priests had arrived. I demanded they carry out their bargain. They laughed in my face. I threw their thirty pieces of silver at their feet and called on the other disciples to join me in fighting for Jesus. But they just ran away in fright. Only Peter drew his sword and even he quickly fled when he saw how outnumbered he was.

I rushed off in anger and fear. I finally came to my special block of land, overlooking the city. There I had hoped to build my palace. It was the perfect spot for a king to live in luxurious majesty, watching his city by day and by night, inviting the rulers of the world to come and pay homage to his majesty.

I hadn't betrayed Jesus. I had wanted him to have the best, to live a quiet and comfortable life with wife, children, money, leisure. He could have had all that if he had done it my way and not alienated the priests the way he did. But he was a wimp. He just let them take him off to the Roman guard, who tortured him and crucified him. And those eleven men

were wimps too—they just ran off and never even
bothered to help him one iota.

Those priests betrayed him. They betrayed me. I
realized that they had used me. Here was I thinking I
had successfully used them in a plan to make myself
king of Israel, and all the time they were working
behind my back to use me to get to Jesus. I had been
prepared to do anything to win, to get to the top, to
be number one. I had been prepared to use anybody,
to lie, steal, plot, twist and turn every which way to
make myself number one.

From my plot of land I looked out over Jerusalem
as dawn was breaking. What could I do now? I realized it was all over. Without the temple priests I
could achieve nothing. I thought about going to
Annas and Caiaphas and offering myself as leader of
their army so we could attack and beat off the
Romans. But I soon realized that that would be
hopeless. They had betrayed Jesus—they had already
betrayed me—they could never be trusted again.
Where could I go? To whom could I turn? I was
alone—hopeless, helpless, with no future at all, no
future at all.

You see me as the one who betrayed Jesus? You have
heard me say how far I was prepared to go in order
to be king. But just you remember this: there is a bit
of me in all of you! There is a bit of me in all of you.

Judas then hanged himself in a tree on his own block
of land—the land on which he had hoped to build his
palace. His ambition hanged him.

And remember too: that "wimp" Jesus is today a
greater king in heaven and earth than Judas ever could
have been. Yes—there's more than a little of Judas in
each one of us.[1]

C⊖NCLUSİ⊖N

What comes through in all these stories of villains is that Jesus did not actively campaign against any of them. He did not try to justify himself when attacked. He pointed to the fact that he always told the truth as God had given it to him. Like Paul after him, he let his life, and the obvious presence and power of God's Spirit in his life, be the only testimony brought into play.

DİSCUSSİ⊖N QUESTİ⊖NS

1. What kinds of troublemakers do you come across in your Christian community? What do you think motivates them?
2. How do you think that you and your leaders should deal with such troublemakers? Is that the way Jesus dealt with those who made trouble for him?
3. How do you and your Christian community balance the needs of individuals against the needs of the whole community?

A Destitute Widow, Weeping Women, and a Prostitute

Jesus was now living through his last days on earth. He had entered Jerusalem, which, for him, was alien territory. As a Galilean, he belonged to the "out-group." John's Gospel highlights this very well: "He came to what was his own, and his own people did not accept him" (John 1:11). He had been sent to Coventry by his fellow house-holders. He was now regarded as an outsider. If you've ever been given the cold shoulder by those whom you love, then you have just a small idea of what it must have been like for the Son of God to be rejected by the very people he came to rescue from their enslavement to sin. Following are three wonderful examples of hope that must have heartened Jesus in those last days. They were like oases in the desert of despair.

We are all too prone to think of Jesus as some kind of superhuman who was impervious to pain, mental anguish, and social rejection. The Gospels report that he gave vent to his anger, and even wept. Anger and sorrow are impossible to those without deep feelings and emotions.

Jesus was very human. Brought up as a typical Mediterranean male, he was subject to all the foibles of his society. Overcoming the prejudices of his day must have been very hard for him. It is no wonder that he often went off on his own to pray. As a man, he needed the help of God to undo a great deal of his upbringing. That does not in any way take away from his divinity. As Paul wrote in Philippians, "he emptied himself, taking the form of a slave, being born in human likeness... and became obedient to the point of death" (Philippians 2:7–8). This is a picture of God taking on the full human nature and voluntarily submitting to the whole human condition, fallen as it was.

Without a concept of a Jesus fully human, warts and all—callused hands and feet, olive skin, hooked nose, volatile nature, body disjointed and wrecked by crucifixion—we will never understand the Jesus alive in each one of us right now. In these three cases, Jesus is relieved for a moment of the despair that must have haunted his last days on earth.

THE DESTİTUTE WİDOW

At the end of more than three years of wandering and teaching around the villages of Galilee, Jesus finally came to Jerusalem, the city of his forefather David. The Gospels tell us that he went straight to the temple and created quite a furor by throwing down the stalls of the money exchangers and driving out the birds and animals sold for the daily sacrifices (Matthew 21:12–17; Mark 11:15–19; Luke 19:45–48; John 2:13–22). Why did Jesus do this?

We need to remember that in those days human labor, rather than money, was the basis of exchange. Goods were bartered on the basis of the time taken to produce them and on the craftsmanship of the artisan, not the money value—"what the market can bear."

Money was introduced by emperors as a way of gathering wealth. Taxes paid in animals, grain, and artifacts don't help to run an empire, build palaces, and increase personal wealth. Human labor and artistry were reduced to dollar values, and all human activities were thereby devalued.

The problem for the Jews was that the Greek and Roman coins to be used in the buying and selling of goods had pagan imagery and inscriptions on them, making them unsuitable for use in the temple. Fortunately, the Romans allowed the Jews to mint their own coins for the temple. Thus, while Roman coins were used to pay taxes and to buy and sell goods where barter was impossible, only temple money could be used to pay the Jews' tithes and other offerings to God.

The money exchangers were allowed to set up their tables in the part of the temple known as the Court of the Gentiles. There, non-Jews were allowed to watch the Jewish rituals and to worship from a distance. Their presence made any area of the temple "out of place," which was why a separate spot was set aside for them. A Jew, wishing to pay his dues, went to an exchanger and haggled over the exchange of his denarii into temple money. The high priests licensed these money men and made themselves quite a fortune out of the exchange fees.

The animal and bird sellers were likewise licensed. Because all offerings had to be perfect, with not a feather or a hair missing, the offerings of worshippers had to be inspected before being accepted. This led, of course, to corruption, so that sometimes even perfect animals were not passed, forcing the worshippers to buy from the sellers there. In the end, most Jews simply purchased a bird or an animal at the temple. This, of course, undermined the whole point of the tithing system, which called for first fruits of crops and firstborn animals that represented the householder's own personal work.

After Jesus turned out the exchangers and sellers— much to the delight of the people—he spent a great deal of time at the temple showing up the absolute hypocrisy of the temple bureaucracy. This, of course, hardly endeared him to the authorities.

During one of these times he and his disciples stood near the offering chests to watch the behavior of the offerers.

> He sat down opposite the treasury, and watched the crowd putting money into the treasury. Many rich people put in large sums. A poor widow came and put in two small copper coins, which are worth a penny. Then he called his disciples and said to them, "Truly I tell you, this poor widow has put in more than all those who are contributing to the treasury. For all of them have contributed out of their abundance; but she out of her poverty has put in everything she had, all she had to live on." (Mark 12:41–44)

The treasury chests were in a prominent place where passersby could look on and see who was giving how much to the temple. The rich men came dressed in their best finery, accompanied by their household slaves. They would stand in front of a chest, hold up their bags of coins for all to see, and ostentatiously drop these into the chests, smiling as the sound of many coins landing gave a message of large amounts. Jesus once satirized these men as those who blew their own trumpets as they deposited their ill-gotten gains into the treasury (Matthew 6:2). No actual trumpets were blown, of course, and Jesus' audience knew it. But they knew exactly what he meant. They had witnessed such behavior many times every day.

The poor, however, tended to come at nonpeak hours and shamefully deposit their few coins so that no one could see how little they could give. But, on this day, one poor, powerless widow turned up among the flaunting

rich. With no family household in which to be embedded,
she had no way of earning her own living except by prostitution. She may have eked out an existence by begging
someplace where not too many male beggars had their spots.
She may have found some housework in return for a meal.

As Jesus and his twelve watched, she went up to the
chest after one of the rich had flaunted his large but
affordable donation. She took out her small leather
money pouch. Untying it, she held it above the chest and
shook it out. Into the chest dropped two copper coins.
Making sure there were no coins left, she rewrapped her
pouch, put it back into her belt, offered her prayer of
thanksgiving to God, and quietly walked away.

The effect of her action was electric. We can imagine
there was a sudden hush from all the onlookers and
those waiting to show off their gifts. Then a low growl
started up as people realized what she had done. Those
two copper coins were leptas: Roman coins, not Jewish
ones. The lepta was of so little value that the temple
authorities had not minted an equivalent for their own
worshippers to use. So, this widow had no option but to
put this dirty money into the treasury, because she didn't
have enough leptas to change into even the smallest
Jewish coin. By giving all she had in the whole world, she
had mixed dirty Roman money with clean Jewish money
and infected that whole chestful of money, making it
out-of-place by association and therefore unfit for offering to God.

One way to visualize this event is to see Jesus jumping
up from his seat, going over to the widow, and giving her
a great bear-hug, at the same time drawing the crowd's
attention to what she had done. He would have told
them all that her two pieces of dirty money, earned by
the sweat of her brow, were of more value to God than
all the clean money that had been extorted from the

poor and tossed so ostentatiously into the treasury
chests. After blessing her and sending her on her way,
he would have gone back and sat with his disciples and
shared this moment of joy. He saw in this widow a sign
of hope for the future, a sign that his life and death
would be worth all the pain and suffering he was
undergoing right there and then. This powerless and
hopeless widow—not temple authorities, scribes,
Pharisees, Sadducees, Herodians, high priests, Levites,
and rich, religious landowners—portrayed the true
nature of discipleship,

This is a reminder to us all of the danger of drawing
too much attention to the gifts and benefactions of the
rich, while giving little credit to those who often have
nothing but their time and energy to devote to the work
of the congregation.

THE MOURNING WOMEN

After his abortive trials, Jesus was led out of the city to
Golgotha to be crucified. He was led along by Roman
soldiers, who had already teased and tortured him. He
no doubt still had the infamous crown of thorns on his
head. He would have been chained to a soldier and his
legs would have been shackled together.

> A great number of the people followed him, and
> among them were women who were beating their
> breasts and wailing for him. But Jesus turned to
> them and said, "Daughters of Jerusalem, do not
> weep for me, but weep for yourselves and for your
> children. For the days are surely coming when they
> will say, 'Blessed are the barren, and the wombs that
> never bore, and the breasts that never nursed.' Then
> they will begin to say to the mountains, 'Fall on us';

and to the hills, 'Cover us.' For if they do this when
the wood is green, what will happen when it is dry?"
(Luke 23:27–31)

As he cringed inwardly at the final torture awaiting
him, he heard the familiar sound of women's voices
raised in mourning. In those days, this mourning cry
symbolized evil, not just death. The women were not just
mourning over the coming death of a loved one; they
were lamenting the evil that was soon to overtake them
all. In publicly bewailing this evil, the women were
breaking the social conventions of their day. Such
mourning should have been kept in their own villages
and households, not cried out publicly in the city of
Jerusalem. No doubt the temple leaders who were part of
this procession ordered them to be quiet. But the more
they were told to be quiet, the louder they keened. The
women knew that this was a triumph of evil over good,
and they gave vent to their feelings.

Finally, Jesus stopped and no doubt asked his captors
to let him put a stop to this mourning. He turned to the
women his ashen, agony-lined face and quietly and lovingly addressed them, "Daughters of Jerusalem!" In using
those words, Jesus affirmed their right to speak their
minds. Women were never recognized as people in their
own right, but only as related to men. "Daughters of the
sons of Jerusalem" would have been socially correct. But
he called them "daughters of Jerusalem"—and used the
word that signified clear blood relationship. He affirmed
their right to speak for themselves in the city to which
they belonged. The temple authorities who were listening
would have been very offended.

He went on, "Do not be lamenting just for me. Lament
for yourselves and your children." Here he was, already
feeling the bite of the nails in his wrists and ankles and

the agony of the torture that would soon put his shoulders, hips, and knees out of joint. And he not only
accepted their lamenting for this terrible evil that was
being wrought, but he urged them to include themselves
and their future generations in their woes.

He warned them about their future. "The days are coming when men will say, 'Blessed are you who are barren,
whose wombs never give birth to new life; and blessed are
you whose breasts never give suck to young babes.'" He
was warning them that their identity as mothers and nur-
turers would be taken from them and replaced by one of
solely sexual instruments for the satisfaction of males.

"The days are coming," he continued, "when you will
bewail your lot so much that you will call down the very
mountains and hills to hide you from the abuse of men."
Then he concluded with words that might be interpreted
to mean, "If right now they will not allow you your right
to mourn and lament for the evil that you see around
you, just imagine what it will be like when I am no
longer with you and you have no one to protect you and
allow you your God-given rights."

We must not see Jesus scolding these women and
telling them to be quiet. Their mourning for the evil that
was befalling him and their city must have been a great
consolation to him, especially as all his twelve had run
off and deserted him. In the midst of the cruelty of
Jerusalem and Rome, these outspoken daughters of
Jerusalem gave him new heart and strength to continue
and see his mission to its bitterest end.

THE PROSTITUTE

Although the following incident is placed early in Luke's
Gospel, it actually occurred later in Jerusalem during
Jesus' last days.

One of the Pharisees asked Jesus to eat with him,
and he went into the Pharisee's house and took his
place at the table. And a woman in the city, who was
a sinner, having learned that he was eating in the
Pharisee's house, brought an alabaster jar of ointment. She stood behind him at his feet, weeping, and
began to bathe his feet with her tears and to dry
them with her hair. Then she continued kissing his
feet and anointing them with the ointment. Now
when the Pharisee who had invited him saw it, he
said to himself, "If this man were a prophet, he
would have known who and what kind of woman
this is who is touching him—that she is a sinner."
Jesus spoke up and said to him, "Simon, I have
something to say to you." "Teacher," he replied,
"Speak." "A certain creditor had two debtors; one
owed five hundred denarii, and the other fifty.
When they could not pay, he canceled the debts for
both of them. Now which of them will love him
more?" Simon answered, "I suppose the one for
whom he canceled the greater debt." And Jesus said
to him, "You have judged rightly." Then turning
toward the woman, he said to Simon, "Do you see
this woman? I entered your house; you gave me no
water for my feet, but she has bathed my feet with
her tears and dried them with her hair. You gave me
no kiss, but from the time I came in she has not
stopped kissing my feet. You did not anoint my head
with oil, but she has anointed my feet with ointment. Therefore, I tell you, her sins, which were
many, have been forgiven; hence she has shown
great love. But the one to whom little is forgiven,
loves little." Then he said to her, "Your sins are forgiven." But those who were at table with him began
to say among themselves, "Who is this who even

forgives sins?" And he said to the woman, "Your
faith has saved you; go in peace." (Luke 7:36–50)

Feasts were an important way of maintaining a man's
honorable standing in the community. At such feasts he
would invite only those men of the same standing as
himself, and he would expect to be invited to feasts in
the homes of those on his guest list. Such eating together
was a way of demonstrating common interests, as well as
establishing networks against common concerns.

The doors and windows of everyone's house were
always open during the day as a way of not only showing
off one's furnishings and table-settings but also proving
that nothing untoward was going on. The whole community would be able to walk by a feast and gossip about
who was there, what they were wearing, and how well
the feast was being catered.

The usual welcoming ceremonies would be carried out
by the household slaves to make sure that no out-of-
place dust was brought inside. Each guest would be taken
to the host for the welcoming kiss on each cheek and
then to his place on the eating couches, where he would
be served with tasty morsels and wine before the main
meal began.

In this case, Simon, a Pharisee, had invited Jesus to this
feast. Did this mean that he regarded Jesus as being on
his same status level? There is no way that an obviously
rich man like Simon, a homeowner, would have accepted
Jesus, an artisan, as his social equal. And by inviting
Jesus, Simon was running the risk that the other men he
had invited would angrily get up and walk out when they
saw a man of a lower class entering the dining room.

But no one did. Why? Jesus gave the clue to this, and to
why Simon had invited him, when he accused Simon of
not offering him the usual welcoming rituals. No slave

had taken off his sandals, washed his feet and hands, and placed slippers on his feet and an outer robe over his shoulders before conducting him to his host for the welcoming kisses and then to his place at the table.

When the other guests saw that Jesus had been taken directly to his place at the lowest end of the seating order without the welcoming rituals, they knew that something was afoot. Simon had planned for Jesus to bring disorder to the feast so that all the guests would have an opportunity to deride him. And Jesus knew it. He knew what he was in for but obediently took his place without a word of complaint. Had he complained to Simon about not being properly welcomed, he would have given Simon the opportunity to start making fun of him in the presence of the other guests.

Fortunately for Jesus, an uninvited guest came straight in and completely derailed Simon's plot. This unnamed prostitute, who had no doubt serviced several of those present at some time or other, knew that Jesus had been invited and guessed what Simon was up to. She knew where to find him in the crowded room and went straight to where he was reclining. She was careful to stand behind him so as not to face him and cause him any offense.

Weeping profusely at this disgraceful treatment of Jesus, she leaned over the back of the couch, took his dusty sandals off, bathed his feet with her tears and dried them with her hair. Her tears, coming out of her eyes, were, according to the Mediterranean mentality, out of place and caused problems of order if they landed on another person's body or clothes. So these tears did not act in the same way as water for bathing feet to get rid of out-of-place dust. Then she kissed Jesus' feet, not his cheeks.

Simon was outraged. This should never have happened in his house. It was bad enough that this prostitute had

gate-crashed his feast and brought his reputation into
serious question, but that she should perform one of her
professional acts on Jesus' body in clear view of both
guests and onlookers out on the street? He could hardly
contain his anger. While he had planned to ridicule Jesus
as a prophet and Messiah by inviting him to this feast, he
certainly would not have planned for this untouchable
woman to do it for him. His only consolation was that
Jesus could not have been a real prophet, since he would
not have allowed this woman to continue in this outra-
geous fashion.

By now, the prostitute had broken the seal on the jar of
valuable ointment she had brought with her and was
anointing Jesus' feet, still weeping. The aroma filled the
whole room and overcame the spicy smell of the food on
the serving tables. The guests were now doubly outraged,
realizing that some of them had probably contributed to
the cost of this very expensive nard, purchased from the
proceeds of her profession.

Before any of them could make a move to rush out in
anger at being so insulted by this woman, Jesus called
them all to attention. Such people loved nothing better
than debating points of law and custom. Jesus put a
question to Simon. "Simon"—notice he didn't name him
as Simon son of whoever his father was. That would have
been the polite and correct form of address. But Jesus
was about to put Simon in his place. "Simon, imagine
that two men owed you money: one five hundred denarii
and the other fifty. And let's say that you decided to cancel
both debts. Tell me: which man would love you more?"

Ordinary people didn't voluntarily borrow money in
those days. They were usually forced into debt as a result
of some calamity, and ended up passing their house and
land over to a rich man who would then demand eighty
or ninety percent of their crop in return for being

allowed to stay there. Perhaps Simon himself got ahold
of some properties in this way. Should a crop fail alto-
gether, it would make good economic sense for the
lender to waive that year's repayment, because otherwise
the debtor would have no assets to make good on the
rent. Having that year's repayment canceled would mean
the debtor would work even harder to show his gratitude
and make even more money for his landlord. Simon
would not have really cared about the man and his family
who had beggared themselves for his benefit.

That was why Simon took the bait Jesus dangled
before him and replied, "I suppose the one who'd had
the bigger debt canceled." But does love result from can-
cellation of debts on good economic grounds? Of course
not! And Simon knew that, which is why he used the
doubt-expressing phrase, "I suppose."

Jesus went on to show how true love is generated. This
woman, forced into prostitution because she had no
male sponsor to give her an identity or a household into
which to be embedded, was expressing to Jesus her pro-
found repentance at her way of life. In using the proceeds of her wicked profession to anoint his feet, she was
pinning her faith on his understanding of her position.
Her out-of-place tears and her sinfully acquired ointment were symbols of the strength of her desire that he
recognize the depth of her remorse at her way of life. She
had not been able to face him, yet she needed his love
and understanding. She was also demonstrating that she
knew what Simon and his guests had intended to do to
shame him. What she had done was to shame Simon by
doing these unthinkable things in his house for all the
guests and the villagers to see.

"Look at her, Simon," Jesus says as he looks her straight
in the face. "You deliberately refused me the normal welcoming ceremonies, even though you had personally

invited me here. But she is more than making up for
your rudeness by washing my feet with her tears and
anointing them with the ointment she purchased with
the only money she had, the proceeds of her sinful profession. She knew she could depend upon my love and
forgiveness, where now, no one in this village will ever be
able to depend upon you to do the right thing by them.

"Simon—she is forgiven, not because she had anything
to gain in coming here and shaming you by expressing
her love for me in this way, but because she proved she
knew she could rely on my love and understanding of
the position your male-dominated society had placed her
in. Yes, Simon, her sins, and yours, are many."

Then Jesus, still looking the prostitute in the face,
spoke to her. "Your sins were many, but they are all forgiven. Because of your faith in me, you have been res-
cued from your life of slavery to prostitution. Go home.
Your life is now back in order."

We are not told what happened next to this prostitute.
But certainly an important part of Jesus' forgiveness of
her would have been the finding of a household for her
so that she need not continue in her profession. God's
forgiveness always has a practical aspect, not just a spiritual and theoretical one.

This wonderful prostitute must have been an oasis in
the desert of denial and failure that surrounded Jesus'
last few days. Whereas community leaders looked only
for the gifts and devotion of those who could add to
their honor, Jesus accepted with gratitude the love and
offerings of an untouchable who could only take away
his honor and shame him.

CONCLUSION

These three events show us how Jesus received encouragement to believe that ultimately his sacrifice would be

worthwhile. If a widow, a group of wailing women, and a prostitute could show him that they had some small glimpse of what he was really about, then imagine what would happen when his sacrifice was completed in his resurrection and ascension to heaven.

It is quite fascinating that, in a world dominated by men, it was left to a small number of women to display real understanding of what was actually going on, and to bring to Jesus some small measure of consolation and hope.

Surely we've all been at our wits' end and wondered whether there was any light at the end of our tunnel. In such cases haven't we treasured the touch of a hand or a quiet hug—gestures of wordless but valuable sympathy? In the same way, Jesus must have treasured these wonderful women as they reached out from their powerlessness and expressed their love and concern for a Messiah who had treated them as individuals in their own right.

DISCUSSION QUESTIONS

1. How do you view problems in your local Christian community? To what extent do you see them as affecting the whole church?
2. To what extent do you value the commitment of the ordinary people, even outcasts, in the overall work of your Christian community?
3. How prepared are you to be there for these ordinary people when they are in need of support?

Joseph of Arimathea, Nicodemus, a Repentant Thief, and a Centurion

I want now to present you with four men who ultimately came to believe that Jesus was who he said he was—God's son and Messiah of Israel.

Joseph of Arimathea

Joseph is unknown outside of the Gospels. His father was not named, but his village of origin was: Arimathea, a town northwest of Jerusalem. It was a very Judean Jewish town, which was probably why Joseph was known by the town's name. He was certainly not a Galilean Jew, and therefore he was part of the Jerusalem in-group.

> Now there was a good and righteous man named Joseph, who, though a member of the council, had not agreed to their plan and action. He came from the Jewish town of Arimathea, and he was waiting expectantly for the kingdom of God. This man went to Pilate and asked for the body of Jesus. Then he took it down, wrapped it in a linen cloth, and laid it in a rock-hewn tomb where no one had ever been laid. (Luke 23:50–53)

Joseph was a member of the Jewish Sanhedrin, the politico-religious governing body of the whole nation to which only rich and influential men ascended. The members were all conservative and under the influence of the high priestly families. Joseph was described as an honorable and righteous man. This was code for a man who kept the law religiously and maintained his status by fulfilling all his duties and benefactions to his community.

Luke described him as a man who disagreed with the decision of the Sanhedrin to manufacture evidence against Jesus in order to get him executed by the Roman government. Luke also says that Joseph "was waiting expectantly for the kingdom of God." By this he implies that Joseph was dissatisfied with the state of the religious establishment and was praying that the visions of the Old Testament prophets concerning the coming of the City of God would be fulfilled in his day.

But according to John, Joseph keep secret his belief in the Messiahship of Jesus (John 19:38), out of his fear of the temple leadership. Although he had hoped that as a member of the Sanhedrin he could bring some influence to bear in saving Jesus, he was unsuccessful. He was to see all his plans, secret discipleship, and careful lobbying go for nothing, as Jesus was led out of the council chambers to Pilate for ratification of the unjust death sentence.

Before the Sabbath was due to begin, Joseph went to Pilate and used his influence as a member of the Sanhedrin to have the body of Jesus taken down from the cross and placed temporarily in his own tomb, hewn out of rock on his own property. No doubt he had in mind erecting a public memorial for Jesus, and in so doing would have risked his own life and position on the Sanhedrin. Thus did a rich and powerful man finally reveal himself as a believer in the Messiahship of Jesus, thereby placing his whole life and honorable position in jeopardy. Certainly he was not allowed to stay on the Sanhedrin.

The apocryphal *Acts of Pilate* sets out details of what happened then to Joseph. He confessed to the Jewish authorities that he had taken the body of Jesus and had laid it in his own tomb. He then accused them of not repenting for having crucified the righteous Jesus. The authorities imprisoned Joseph in a cell without windows and set a guard over him until the day after the coming Sabbath. When they arrived to carry him off for execution, they discovered that he had disappeared. From then on they were afraid to imprison any of the other disciples of Jesus.[2]

NICODEMUS

Another secret disciple was Nicodemus. His name means "victor over the people," thus placing him squarely in the ruling classes. He was not only a member of the Sanhedrin but was also a synagogue leader. He is mentioned only in John's Gospel as the one who came to Jesus by night.

Now there was a Pharisee named Nicodemus, a leader of the Jews. He came to Jesus by night and said to him, "Rabbi, we know that you are a teacher who has come from God; for no one can do these signs that you do apart from the presence of God." Jesus answered him, "Very truly, I tell you, no one can see the kingdom of God without being born from above." Nicodemus said to him, "How can anyone be born after having grown old? Can one enter a second time into the mother's womb and be born?" Jesus answered, "Very truly, I tell you, no one can enter the kingdom of God without being born of water and Spirit. What is born of the flesh is flesh, and what is born of the Spirit is spirit. Do not be astonished that I said to you, 'You must be born from above.' The wind blows where it chooses, and you hear the sound of it, but you do not know where it comes from or where it goes. So it is with everyone who is born of the Spirit." Nicodemus said to him, "How can these things be?" Jesus answered him, "Are you a teacher of Israel, and yet you do not understand these things?

Very truly, I tell you, we speak of what we know and testify to what we have seen; yet you do not receive our testimony. If I have told you about earthly things and you do not believe, how can you believe if I tell you about heavenly things? No one has ascended into heaven except the one who descended from heaven, the Son of Man. And just as Moses lifted up the serpent in the wilderness, so must the Son of Man be lifted up, that whoever believes in him may have eternal life." (John 3:1–15)

The only time Nicodemus could have confronted Jesus in other than a challenging way would have been at night, when doors and windows were closed. As a member of the ruling establishment, he would have been expected to challenge Jesus in public in order to put him down. He was, after all, of superior status to Jesus. He would never have addressed Jesus as "Rabbi" in public, because that would have been to defer to him as superior; nor would he have called Jesus "a teacher," because that would have indicated that Jesus had some rabbinical training. The Sanhedrin always labeled Jesus as ignorant of the law in order to put him down before the people.

Nicodemus admitted that Jesus had performed many "signs," a word John used to show that Jesus had established that the origin of his teaching was from God, making

him different from earlier freedom fighters. Nicodemus
was challenged to establish whether he relied only upon
his obedience to God's law for his membership in the
kingdom of God or whether he had been transformed
from the inside by God's Spirit. This was the single factor
that distinguished Jesus' teaching from that of all other
religious teachers. Jesus declared that membership in the
kingdom of God resulted solely from inner spiritual
change accomplished by an outside force—God's Spirit.
Judaism, like Islam later, relied solely on human effort to
achieve perfect law keeping.

We don't know how Nicodemus reacted to all of this.
But we do know that on one occasion, when the temple
police went to arrest Jesus, Nicodemus risked his neck by
protesting at the injustice of not giving Jesus a proper
legal hearing. He was quickly put in his place by being
called a Galilean who did not know the law. "Surely you
are not also from Galilee, are you? Search and you will see
that no prophet is to arise from Galilee" (John 7:50–52).

Being called a Galilean was just like being called an
ignorant fool today. We last see Nicodemus joining
Joseph of Arimathea in begging the body of Jesus from
Pilate and contributing to Jesus' embalming with a huge
amount of costly ointment.

We know nothing about the later life of Nicodemus. A
gospel was invented for him, and the *Acts of Pilate* (XV.1)
tries to show him as a Scripture scholar.

In these two powerful, high-status men we have examples of secret discipleship from within the establishment
that murdered Jesus, a discipleship that in many ways
was more committed than that of the apostles.

THE PENITENT THIEF

When Jesus was crucified, two criminals were crucified
with him, one on either side. Variously described as robbers

or evildoers, they must have committed something more offensive than robbery to be given the death sentence, unless they robbed from the temple. When one of them berated the other and said, "We are receiving the due reward of our deeds," he was admitting that they had done something serious enough to warrant crucifixion.

Crucifixion was a dirty, smelly, and cruel form of execution, designed to give maximum satisfaction to viewers. The French Revolution's beheadings pale in contrast. You might like to read Psalm 22 and see how closely the details there match what happened to Jesus.

The Roman soldiers had become experts in crucifixion, a combination of torture and execution. This is how crucifixion was carried out: The cross was laid flat on the ground just at the edge of the hole into which it would eventually be hoisted. The criminal was entirely stripped of clothing, which was the main reason that Jews labeled those who had been crucified as "shamed" and "cursed." Public nakedness was always shameful. Then the criminal's legs were crossed at the ankles and a long metal nail driven through them just above the ankles. The position of this nail was quite important. The aim was to leave the body slightly bent, so that when the wrists were nailed to the crossbeam, the weight of the body would put pressure on the ankles. Then the arms were stretched out and nails driven through the arms just near the wrists. The cross was then raised up and its end driven into the hole. It was fixed there with stones to make sure that it did not fall over because of the jerking of the body.

In Jesus' case, the temple authorities wanted the written charge against Jesus nailed above his head for all to see: "Jesus of Nazareth who said he was king of the Jews." Pilate, of course, left out two important words, so that it read, "Jesus of Nazareth, the king of the Jews." Pilate had to have the last laugh, making sure, by having it written

in Hebrew, Greek and Latin, that all passersby understood the charge (John 19:19–23).

Very soon the process of crucifixion started to take its
toll. It was designed as a very visual event. The victim
tried to ease the pain in his ankles and take the weight
on his wrists by pulling his body up from the nail in his
ankles. Then he had to relieve the pain in his wrists by
letting his body droop and take the weight on his ankles.
The time between these actions got rapidly shorter until
there was a constant movement up and down. Soon
blood, bodily fluids, and excreta poured out of the body's
orifices, almost totally draining the body of all its fluids.

This continued for several hours until the heart finally
gave out from stress and shock. Sometimes wine mixed
with a drug was poured into the victim's mouth, not to
deaden the pain but to reduce the shock and make the
process last longer. In the meantime, the victim's shoulders, elbows, hips, and knees became disjointed. Because
the Sabbath was soon to begin, the Roman soldiers came
and broke the legs of the two criminals by hitting them
hard with hammers. This hastened their deaths by
adding to the shock.

Sometime into their crucifixion, one of the two criminals in his agony railed at Jesus, demanding that he work
one of his alleged miracles and get them down:

> One of the criminals who hanged there kept derid-
> ing him and saying, "Are you not the Messiah? Save
> yourself and us!" But the other rebuked him, saying,
> "Do you not fear God, since you are under the same
> sentence of condemnation? And we indeed have
> been condemned justly, for we are getting what we
> deserve for our deeds, but this man has done noth-
> ing wrong." Then he said, "Jesus, remember me
> when you come into your kingdom." He replied,

"Truly I tell you, today you will be with me in
Paradise." (Luke 23:39–43)

The other criminal, in a moment of enlightenment,
told his fellow criminal to be quiet and show some sense
of God's justice. They were getting their just deserts,
whereas the man between them was innocent of any
crime and was being tortured unjustly. He then forced
his head around so that he could look at Jesus, jerking in
agony beside him. "Jesus, remember me when you come
into your kingdom!" What on earth caused this criminal
to suddenly realize who Jesus really was? What brought
him to his senses? Remember, he was a criminal who had
committed a capital offense.

Two things could account for the criminal's insight: he
realized that Jesus was not an angel in human appear-
ance but actually a human being who was suffering what
he was suffering, and he saw that Jesus in his agony did
not berate his accusers and God. The criminal would
have heard Jesus say, "Father forgive them, for they do
not know what they are doing" (Luke 23:34). He would
have heard Jesus recite the opening words of Psalm 22,
"My God, My God, why have you forsaken me?" (Mark
15:34) and would have remembered the rest of the Psalm
that he himself had chanted many times at synagogue as
a young man—and its final words of the triumph of the
Messiah. Perhaps, in his agony, he put these things
together and sensed that Jesus was the Messiah promised
in the Scriptures.

No matter. He turned to Jesus and did not ask to be
relieved of the rest of the punishment he was due for his
crimes, but asked simply to be remembered as one who
had come to his senses too late to make amends for his
transgressions. Jesus, in the midst of his own agony,
turned to him and managed to get out these words: "I

am telling you this on my own honor: this very day you
will join me in paradise."

And right then, writes Luke, as if in judgment on all
who were there, God darkened the world so no one
could see the rest of the agony of the Son of God and the
two criminals beside him (Luke 23:44–45).

Can we truly appreciate how Jesus must have felt when
that criminal put his trust in him? The whole nation and
the entire religious establishment, to whom Jesus had
come to announce God's coming kingdom, had rejected
him and executed him as a criminal, but this one criminal had turned from his evil ways and entrusted himself
to him.

THE CENTURION

The detachment of Roman soldiers who had so efficiently
carried out the execution ignored the sights and sounds
of the victims on their crosses. This was familiar to them,
used, as they were, to death and torture. They had
already had their fun at Jesus' expense, dressing him up
as a king and playing blind man's bluff with him.

They filled in the rest of their time playing with dice to
see who would get Jesus' one-piece caftan, lovingly hand-
crafted by his mother. The darkness stopped their game
and one of them won the caftan. The chief priests went to
the centurion in charge and demanded that the three victims be killed and their bodies taken down as the Sabbath
was due to start. Dead bodies on crosses on the Sabbath
would be sacrilege. That the Son of God himself was
hanging there at their behest was not sacrilege, of course!

Heaving a sigh of relief that they could soon get back
to their barracks and their prostitutes, two of the soldiers
grabbed their large hammers and slammed the thighs
and knees of the two criminals to shatter their bones and

hasten their deaths. As they moved to Jesus, they found, to their astonishment, that he had stopped writhing and was no longer breathing. One of them picked up a lance and thrust it into Jesus' left side just to be doubly sure. And from the pierced heart rushed blood that had already separated into plasma and liquid, a sure sign of death.

The centurion had already seen Jesus breathe his last. He had not taken part in the gambling for Jesus' caftan but had been watching him carefully. He had heard all of Jesus' words, including those to the criminal and his very last ones, "Father, into your hands I commend my spirit" (Luke 23:46).

According to Luke, the centurion, when he saw what had taken place, praised God and exclaimed, "Certainly this man was innocent" (Luke 23:47). According to Matthew and Mark he said, "Truly, this man was God's Son" (Matthew 27:54; Mark 15:39). And Luke alone writes that "when all the crowds who had gathered there for the spectacle saw what had taken place, they returned home, beating their breasts" (Luke 23:48), a sign that they regretted their part in the murder of an innocent man.

Thus do two secret disciples from among the religious ruling classes, a criminal, and a battle-hardened Roman centurion acknowledge Jesus as Messiah, while the religious establishment is self-satisfied at having, they thought, gotten rid of Jesus forever.

DISCUSSION QUESTIONS

1. How difficult is it to present the claims of Christ to political, legal, and academic leaders?
2. What examples do you know of "people in high places" who profess to be followers of Christ?
3. To what extent do your neighbors and community leaders know about your personal commitment to Christ and the church?

THE CRUCIFIXION OF JESUS AND US

The previous chapter outlines the way in which crucifixion was actually carried out. A brutal form of torture invented by the Romans, it was used not only as a disincentive to crime but also as entertainment for the masses. The Roman satirist Juvenal once commented that "the people that once bestowed commands, consulships, legions, and all else, now concerns itself no more, and longs eagerly for just two things—bread and circuses."[3] One of the "circuses" was public crucifixion.

One way that I found to help us all come to grips with the reality of the crucifixion that Jesus, innocent of any crimes against Rome, had to endure was to present the following meditation during the Good Friday service. I myself, and many who were present, found it to be a life-changing experience.

The meditation is based on a hymn many of us sing during Lent, "When I Survey the Wondrous Cross," which was written by Isaac Watts, the seventeenth-century English hymn writer responsible for many hymns still sung today. What I have done in this meditation is to show that Watts, while trying to place the crucifixion at the center of our faith, has overidealized and overspiritualized it to the extent of removing, almost completely, the reality of Jesus' suffering. So much of our art in stained-glass windows and icons makes the cross easier

for us to look at—even to admire—resulting in our
missing its brutality and shame.

When I conducted this meditation, I sang the words
from Isaac Watts' hymn, but you may choose to simply
say the words or to have someone else say or sing them.

I organized a rough, simple wooden cross to stand on
the altar. When the time came to present the meditation,
I went first to the altar, took the cross and carried it to
the top of the chancel stairs. There I placed it next to the
place where I would speak. This allowed me to point to
the cross from time to time.

I usually dressed in simple black clothes rather than
ecclesiastical robes.

A MEDİTATİON FOR GOOD FRİDAY

(Take the cross from the altar and place it beside you.)

"When I survey the wondrous…"

(Stop short.)

The wondrous cross? Just look at it, standing on the
floor there.

(Point to the cross and look at it.)

Two huge beams of rough timber, already blood-
soaked from countless previous victims, eagerly awaiting
the next victim's life blood.

"Wondrous cross"? What's "wondrous" about being
dragged onto that vertical beam?

Watch, as the grinning Roman soldier holds the victim
down with a heavy foot planted on his bare stomach.
Watch as another Roman soldier stretches out the right

arm along the horizontal beam, while a third positions
the giant metal nail over the center of the wrist, and a
fourth raises a massive wooden mallet and with one
practiced stroke slams the nail through the wrist into the
wood. Watch as three of the soldiers take the victim's left
arm and nail it to the other side of the horizontal beam,
making sure that the victim's arms are stretched as far
apart as possible.

Watch as the soldiers move to the victim's feet.
They take the right leg and force the foot up a few
inches so that the knee is lightly bent. While the heel
is forced to the other side of the vertical beam, the
soldiers position the large metal nail just above the
ankle and driven through the bone until it just breaks
through to the wood. They then place the left ankle
under the right one and batter the nail through until
it is well into the wood.

They lever the cross upright into a deep hole in the
ground. The hole has enough room in it to allow the
cross to move around with the fevered convulsing and
shaking of the victim without toppling over. This is what
the voyeurs have come to watch.

"When I survey that bloody cross on which the Prince
of glory…"

(*Stop short.*)

"Prince"? "Prince of Glory"?

(*Point to the cross.*)

Just look at him now on that bloody cross. Forget
those artistic paintings with their carefully positioned
drapes hiding his manhood. This Prince is stark naked.

Look at his head. No golden, jewel-encrusted crown of office on that head. A wreath of jagged green thorn-bush roughly forced down to his ears, gouging out great hunks of flesh and hair on the way down.

Look at his right hand. No golden ring of royal descent on that finger, already bleeding from the military beating received at the barracks. No royal purple robe, just the skin in which he was born thirty-three years ago, much abused by Pilate's orders and the manhandling of the military police. The Romans never treated their own princes like that. They gave them a bowl of poison and told them to go home and drink it. Never such a public execution as this for their own.

They did this to the Son of God.

(*Turn again to the congregation.*)

"When I survey that bloody Cross
   On which the Son of God was reviled
My richest gain I count but loss,
   And pour contempt on all my pride."

What gain for me—what pride in me—can there possibly be when I survey that bloody cross? How can I possibly compare my contemptible pride in my own petty achievements and the thoughts of revenge I harbor against those who plot against me, to the way the Son of God prays to his heavenly Father for his executioners, who are so obviously enjoying their ghastly duty. "Father, forgive them," he says, "for they do not know what they are doing." Especially when they did know exactly what they were doing, having done it many times before.

But how could they know the implications of their work, even when their commander knew whom they were executing—didn't he say, "Surely this man was the Son of God"? Where is pride in any human achievement

when the Son of God failed so miserably? Where is the
pride of position and office? How can prelates and popes
and patriarchs so boastfully display their position and
authority while pretending it all came from the Son of
God on this bloody cross? How can huge eighteen-carat
gold crucifixes, bastardizing, romanticizing, and deni-
grating this ghastly sight with opulence, adorn their
puffed-up breasts and their multimillion dollar edifices?
How truly contemptible is the human deconstruction
and reconstruction of that cross!

And those Roman soldiers are so bored by the whole
thing that they gamble away the hours over the Son of
God's only worldly possession, the one-piece, hand-
woven robe so lovingly made by his mother, now sobbing
her heart out at the monstrous sight of her innocent
son's passion.

> "See from His head, His hands, His feet,
>   Sorrow and love flow mingled down;"

(*Stop short.*)

What arrant nonsense, Isaac Watts! How dare you pen
such blasphemy! Not sorrow and love flowing down, but
blood, Isaac—genuine, red, human gore, mixed with
feverish, painful, and stinking sweat!

Look again at that bloody cross.

(*Point to the cross on the floor.*)

Within minutes the victim's shoulders are dislocated
by the force of the muscular contractions caused by the
fierce pain and the unnatural position of the body. The
victim shifts his weight from ankles to wrists, from wrists
to ankles, trying to relieve the fierce and relentless agony.

Blood and heavy, fear-smelly sweat flow down those limbs. And then, what the crowd has been waiting for: the involuntary emptying of the body's store of waste.

"Did e'er such blood and torture meet,
    And thorns gouge deep, and pity drown."

Just once—once in a lifetime—let us face the grim reality of this very cross. Let us face all that the Son of God went through to bring us back to the God who loves us, the God from whom we have strayed, the God who has handed on to us the very mission that Jesus began: "As the Father has sent me, so I have sent you."

We need to get our own lives—our pain and our joy—into perspective. We all complain too much when things go wrong, when we find no satisfaction in life, when nothing seems to be achieved no matter how hard we try to obey God. Just this once, let us see deeply into exactly what happened on that Good Friday.

"Were the whole realm of nature mine,
    That were an offering…"

(*Stop short.*)

An offering? Isaac Watts, you've really got it messed up now! What made you think Jesus wanted an offering from us? Is that why he went through all that agony and public debasement—to receive offerings from those whose place he took on that cross?

We can't even begin to think how to make up to Jesus for what he went through! But that's not the point, is it? Look again at that cross.

(*Point to the cross on the floor.*)

The other two are on their crosses, writhing and
screaming in pain. They are blaming Jesus for their
agony and punishment, just as in every age people blame
God for all their pain and suffering: "Why has God let
this happen to me?" "Why doesn't God do something?"

And then one of the crucified thieves suddenly sees the
light. "We deserve everything we are getting, but this
man has done nothing wrong and here he is in unjust
agony, being treated as one of us. Lord, please remember
that in the end I stopped blaming you for my crimes."

And right there, on that cruel cross, the innocent Son
of God made him this precious promise: "This very day
you will walk beside me in the new garden of Eden."

There was nothing asked of this repentant criminal—
no offering demanded, no thanks required, no obei-
sance, no acts of penance, no lighting of candles or
washing of feet. The moment that thief stopped blaming
God for his own sinfulness, accepted the just punishment for his own crimes, and was prepared to accept
whatever the Son of God had in store for him—that
very moment he was assured of a place beside Jesus in
the new Garden of Eden.

That thief went on in his agony. Jesus did not wave a
magic wand and get rid of the pain or summon the
angels to take him off the cross and fly him up to
Abraham's bosom. But that thief had the certainty that
he could take the suffering, because now he had something to live for—he had a future. He was not asking that
God treat him better than the Son of God.

Look at that cross again.

(*Point to the cross.*)

Mary, mother of the crucified Jesus, needs a suitable
male to care for her now her eldest son is about to die.

Ancient society did not treat single, unattached women and widows at all well. In the midst of his agony, Jesus thought to make sure she was looked after by his disciple John. "Woman, here is your son: son, here is your mother."

Isaac Watts—who was giving offerings to whom?

All Jesus asks is that we stop blaming God for the way we humans are ruining this planet, that we stop blaming God for the consequences of our own misdeeds, that we stop asking God to do something about the governments we elect and the partners we marry and the children we beget and the careers we choose and the messes we make for ourselves—and accept our place on that cross next to the cross of Jesus.

The offering we receive from God is our own unique and special place beside Jesus in the redeemed Garden of Eden, and the courage to take up our cross and follow him to that place.

"Were the whole realm of nature mine,
    To take and keep me free from care,
I'd rather share in Jesus' pain,
    And evermore my cross to bear."

(Go
and
stretch
out
on the floor in the form of
a
cross
beside
the
cross,
face
down.)

This concludes these studies in which I have tried to highlight some of the key people who featured in Jesus' last days as a human being in Jerusalem. I have tried to emphasize the humanness, not only of these people, but also of Jesus himself. By doing this I hope that we will all have some sense of the truth that "we were there, too." If he died for us, then we were there, either on the side of the religious establishment who were intent on his murder or among those who came to believe that he is who he claimed to be, the Son of God and Redeemer of the whole world.

I believe that it is good for us all, each Lent, to take ourselves back to Jerusalem, to the hill of the Cross, and to stand and watch Jesus die for us. Hopefully, we will thus catch a vision of the kind of people Jesus still needs today to help him in the ongoing work of the redemption of the whole world.

NOTES

1. The Gospel accounts of Judas are contained
   in: Matthew 26:14–16, 26:25, 26:47–50,
   27:3–10; Mark 14:10–11, 14:43–46; Luke
   22:3–6; John 18:2–5; Acts 1:16–20.

2. Acts of Pilate XII.1–2 in *New Testament
   Apocrypha*, ed. Hennecke and Schneemelcher,
   tr. Wilson (Louisville, Kentucky: Westminster
   John Knox Press, 1963).

3. Juvenal. *The Sixteen Satires* X.l.79, tr. Green
   (Harmondsworth: Penguin, 1967).

4. The Gospel accounts of the crucifixion of
   Jesus are contained in: Matthew 27:32–56;
   Mark 15:21–41; Luke 23:26–49; and John
   19:17–37.